Henry M. Morris

Father of Modern Creationism

ICR

INSTITUTE FOR
CREATION
RESEARCH

Henry M. Morris

Father of Modern Creationism

BY

REBECCA MORRIS BARBER

INSTITUTE FOR
CREATION
RESEARCH

Dallas, Texas
ICR.org

Henry M. Morris
Father of Modern Creationism
by Rebecca Morris Barber

First printing: June 2017

All Scripture quotations are from the King James Version.

ISBN: 978-1-935587-83-5
Library of Congress Catalog Number: 2017942271

Please visit our website for other books and resources: ICR.org

Printed in the United States of America.

Contents

Foreword

Many people have come up to me during the Institute for Creation Research's seminars and conferences, sharing about their special moments with my father—never speaking of him as "Henry" or "Dr. Henry," always with the well-earned honorific of "Dr. Morris." It often reminds me of an old story we've recounted in the family for years.

When my brother John and I worked for ICR and Christian Heritage College in El Cajon, California, our mother phoned in one day and asked the receptionist if she could speak to Dr. Morris. The regular receptionist was out for a few days, and a substitute young lady was filling in for her on the switchboard. The new receptionist did not recognize mother's voice and politely answered,

"Certainly ma'am, which Dr. Morris did you wish to speak to?" (Both John and I had also earned doctor's degrees.)

Now, my mother was a most gracious lady, and did not want to embarrass the young receptionist, so she responded to her:

"Well, you know, the one who writes books."

By this time in our lives, both John and I were also published authors, so the receptionist politely repeated,

"Yes ma'am, but which Dr. Morris are you referring to?"

"The one who speaks for ICR," mother said (a little irked that she had not yet been understood). Once again, both John and I were very active on ICR's seminar circuit during this time.

"Of course, ma'am," the receptionist replied, "but there are three Dr. Morrises at ICR and the college—which one would you like me to connect you to?"

Well, by this time mother (who had raised six children and was used to "instant" obedience from them) was more than a little irritated.

"I want to speak to the *real* Dr. Morris!"

That title took! As the firstborn of six children, I have known the "real" Dr. Morris as a godly father, a keen scholar, a Bible teacher, a respected colleague, and finally as a dear friend. In all of these relationships I have come to realize that my mother's somewhat exasperated comment is, perhaps, the best way to remember him.

The "real" Dr. Morris was unique and irreplaceable during his lifetime. His vision to reach many for Christ drove him to battle the devil's lie of evolutionary naturalism and to stand firm against the awful drift from the accuracy and authority of God's Word in the churches and Christian educational institutions. No doubt, many thousands of people have been encouraged by his communication with them in the pulpits, conferences, and seminars over the decades. Perhaps many more have been helped through his writings.

This short biography of Dr. Henry M. Morris Jr. (H.M. to those who were close to him) is more than a list of things done over time, but a very personal look into the life of a man God chose for an unusual task. Like many leaders, the life needed molding into a "vessel unto honour" that would become "sanctified, and meet for the master's use, and prepared unto every good work" (2 Timothy 2:21).

You will find that our little sister Rebecca has done a terrific job researching the huge volume of letters, notes, pictures, and testimonies—kind words from the hundreds of people who have recorded the impact that our earthly father left on them.

The trail of his ministry runs long and deep across the world, and the trophies of his testimony will bear fruit for generations to come. But his major legacy is the Institute for Creation Research. ICR and the work accomplished by the scientists and educators that Dr. Morris recruited to share his passion have spawned hundreds of advocates for a creationist worldview. This institute has been the mother ship that birthed several organizations to expand the vision he embraced.

You will find much in this short book. Some incidents you will identify with, some will touch your heart, and some will make you laugh. Throughout the chapters you will see God's hand in this story and, I trust, it will encourage you to keep trusting God during the challenges in your own life.

But most of all, you will come to know the "real" Dr. Morris and find in his life and legacy the genuine humility and godly faithfulness that makes a man "his workmanship, created in Christ Jesus unto good works, which God hath before ordained that we should walk in them" (Ephesians 2:10).

Henry M. Morris III
Chief Executive Officer
Institute for Creation Research

Preface

Henry M. Morris Jr., my father, wrote a short autobiography for his family to enjoy with the instructions that it was not to be published as written. The manuscript has never been edited or changed and will not be published. However, he knew and expected even then that the material would be used for the purpose of bringing glory to God. It is with that intent that some of his unedited paragraphs are included in this story. He wrote another manuscript on child rearing to provide insight for his children, who were then raising his grandchildren. Likewise, this will not be published, but excerpts are included in this book. I've also included letters, poetry, and other communications by Henry Morris with the hope that each will truly bring honor to our great God who orchestrated his life.

Prologue

When Dr. Henry M. Morris Jr. went to be with the Lord on February 25, 2006, even critics acknowledged his fierce intellect, impeccable character, and enormous influence. Staunch evolutionist Kenneth Miller said, "I found Morris to be unfailingly polite, a real gentleman and a person who was a sincere and committed Christian." Edward Larson, author of *Evolution: The Remarkable History of a Scientific Theory*, said of Morris, "He had an enormous influence. He literally set the terms of the debate for the second half of the 20th century." Friend and foe alike unanimously regard him as the Father of Modern Creationism.

He wrote over 60 books that wove together theology and science, nearly all of them written by hand on yellow notepads. He participated in high-profile creation/evolution debates and led seminars and conferences all over the world. He formed groundbreaking scientific explanations for creation and the Flood, and his book *The Genesis Flood*, co-written with Dr. John Whitcomb, was a primary catalyst for much of the modern biblical creationism movement. Passionate in personal evangelism, Dr. Morris distributed thousands of Bibles to soldiers and college students through his involvement with the Gideons and helped form two Gideon chapters. He also started a church out of his home and teamed up with Dr. Tim LaHaye to found a college and a Christian book publishing company. He helped form a creation society for scientists and other professionals, a leading biblical creation institute, a Christian apologetics graduate program, and an organization that provides creation science accreditation for schools, colleges, and universities. Though the names may have changed, every one of these institutions endures to this day.

He received thousands of letters—and personally responded to nearly all of them. Later in life, when he was President of the Institute for Creation Research, he kept many of these letters in a file cabinet. Not far from his old wooden desk, a plaque hung always within view, "Perhaps Today!"

> Perhaps today is the day of salvation, perhaps today is the day of some breakthrough, perhaps today is the day to go home to the Lord, perhaps today the Lord will return.[1]

With such a perspective, Dr. Morris kept his focus on the things that matter for eternity. A review of his life reveals his reluctance to waste one moment or utter one idle word. His passion for the truth was an example to his family and all who knew him.

He is called the Father of Modern Creationism, but he would firmly deny it. He would say the modern creation revival was the result of God moving in individual hearts to recognize the truth that Scripture represents. Nevertheless, he was one man whom God chose to put voice and pen to that truth. Dr. Henry Morris' life shows how God can take our broken stories and struggles and use us for His kingdom in ways we could have never imagined.

Though he often felt inadequate and ill at ease in such a

public position, he never wavered when the call to arms went out. His voice never faltered when the inerrancy of God's Word was challenged. In this one humble and gentle man, God provided a champion to wield the two-edged sword of His powerful and perfect Word.

Christians clearly understood Dr. Morris' apologetics and followed him into the battle. His legacy lives on in those who continue to proclaim the supreme authority of the Bible to a compromising church and unbelieving culture.

Morris Family Tree

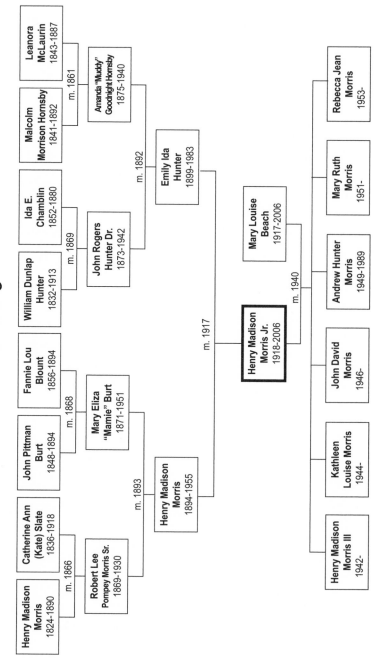

1
Prayer Changes Things

Every now and then, an event occurs that changes the spiritual journey of its witnesses. One such event occurred in the life of a baby who grew up to influence a multitude of Christians in their understanding of God's Word. This child's spiritual journey began in an Army camp in Texas with the prayer of a godly man.

Henry Madison Morris Jr.—later known as H.M. to family, friends, and acquaintances—was born October 6, 1918, near the end of World War I to Henry Madison Morris Sr. and Ida Morris. Our heavenly Father had big plans for this young family and engineered a series of events that eventually touched the lives of thousands.

H.M.'s parents came from well-to-do Texan families. Emily Ida Hunter, known as Ida, was born in Hornsby's Bend in Texas to John Rogers Hunter, a country doctor, and Amanda Goodnight Hornsby Hunter, the daughter of a prominent pioneer family. Dr. Hunter was an avid gun collector who kept a pet bear chained in the backyard. The Hunters and their two daughters, Vivian and Ida, lived in a beautiful Victorian home. As seen in a few surviving photographs, Ida's childhood seemed to reflect the gentle and gracious style of a prosperous country family.

In 1910, Ida's family relocated to El Paso, Texas, a border town renowned for its untamed frontier spirit, where her father began a medical practice. He became active in the Masons, calling it his "religion." The medical practice thrived, and the family enjoyed a lifestyle of comfortable wealth. Dr. Hunter acquired luxury automobiles, while Amanda and her daughters mingled in the town's high society.

Ida mastered the piano as a teen, performing at social events, entertaining at ladies' teas, playing "rags" for dances, and even accompanying the orchestra when the New York Metropolitan

John Rogers Hunter, country doctor

Ida Hunter's childhood home

Company came to town. After high school, Ida and her friends made several outings in her father's touring cars. Her photographs of these trips reveal a girl with a quirky sense of humor and a penchant for adventure. In an era of new freedom for the young, her photos, scrapbooks, dance cards, and club parties tell of a lifestyle of ease and fun.

In 1910, the family of Robert Lee Pompey Morris moved to El Paso. Robert Lee had owned a saloon but was at the time involved in oil lease investments. He, like every other man in that lively border town, "packed a pistol." His oldest son was

Ida and friends in Deming, New Mexico

Fun times

21

Henry Senior, the namesake of his grandfather. The Morris family was also well-to-do, and Henry Senior's name appeared often in the high society news.

Ida and Henry Senior met soon after high school, sparking a romance. On May 9, 1917, they said their vows at a quiet and unattended ceremony in the home of Ida's Baptist pastor. Her wedding book noted, "Not even mother was there," and judging from the entry that said Harriet, her best friend, "even refused to see us until two or three days afterwards," one must suspect that it was a rather sudden decision.

One might think that with such a start the chances for influence from the light of the gospel would be dim. The young wife, Ida, was brought up in a Christian home, but shortly after her marriage her parents separated and ultimately divorced.

Henry Senior's mother, Mamie, was a devoted Christian and tried to raise her family for the Lord, but his father and siblings rarely attended church. Henry Senior made a public

statement to follow Jesus as a boy in a revival meeting under evangelist Mordecai Ham, but as a young adult he claimed he would quit church as soon as he was out of the house.

Henry Senior and Ida (left); Henry Senior, Ida, and friends (right)

The young groom had many worldly examples in his family to follow. Henry Senior's brother and uncle were saloon keepers, and this association carried some influence. His grandfather and namesake, the first Henry Madison Morris (known by the family as "Prime"), served as a sergeant in Company A, 8th Mississippi Infantry for the Confederate Army during the Civil War. He had a wife and multiple children but after the war either divorced or abandoned his family and married a widow, raising another family of four children. Divorce—in an era where it was considerably less common than today—appeared in every generation of this family, with all its resulting bitterness and regret.

The United States entered World War I in 1917, and Henry Senior enlisted and trained in Demming, New Mexico. Shortly after being transferred to a military station in the Dallas area, Henry Senior and Ida moved to North Bishop Street in a suburb of the city, and H.M. was born.

H.M. Morris

At the time of H.M's birth, Henry Senior was stationed at Camp Bowie in Texas. R.A. Torrey—Christian evangelist, pastor, educator, and author—was also serving there. His accomplishments with the Bible Institute of the Chicago Evangelization Society (now Moody Bible Institute), Church of the Open Door in Los Angeles, and the Bible Institute of Los Angeles (now Biola University) are well known, and he preached in evangelistic crusades all over the world. Torrey was also deeply committed to the practice of persistent prayer. Dr. Will Houghton, preaching at his funeral, said:

> But those who knew Dr. Torrey more intimately knew him as a man of regular and uninterrupted prayer. He knew what it meant to pray without ceasing. With hours set systematically apart for prayer, he gave himself diligently to this ministry.[1]

The Torrey-Alexander Mission at the Albert Hall

Torrey himself, speaking of Christ's ministry of intercession on behalf of believers, said,

If we then are to have fellowship with Jesus Christ in His present work, we must spend much time in prayer; we must give ourselves to earnest, constant, persistent, sleepless, overcoming prayer. I know of nothing that has so impressed me with a sense of the importance of praying at all seasons, being much and constantly in prayer, as the thought that that is the principal occupation at present of my risen Lord. I want to have fellowship with Him, and to that end I have asked the Father that whatever else He may make me, to make me at all events an intercessor, to make me a man who knows how to pray, and who spends much time in prayer.[2]

Torrey took time out of his international ministry, at the age of 61, to act as chaplain at the camp. The chaplain happened to drop by Ida's house, and R. A. Torrey took the infant H.M. from his mother's arms, prayed over him, and dedicated him to the Lord's service. Little did they know how God would specifically answer his prayer and work in wondrous ways to preserve and prepare this child for a unique ministry—one that established and built the faith of countless Christians.

2

The Spirit Calls

H. M.'s spiritual leanings did not come from his parents or immediate family. His mother was accustomed to privilege, Christian in name and practice but frivolous and rebellious. His father was determined to pursue wealth but had a propensity for alcohol, gambling, and the secular lifestyle of the Masons. Both led the family into insecurity, dysfunction, and failure.

Henry Senior and sister (left); Henry Senior as Shriner (right)

His ancestors carried the name "Christian" as well, yet the recorded history shows little evidence of a lifestyle committed to Christian principles. As mentioned in the last chapter, his great-grandfather and namesake, Prime, had two families. Married to Emily Cantwell and the father of nine sons in Mississippi, he joined the infantry during the Civil War. He and his family survived the war, but by 1866 he married another woman, Catherine Slate. There is no record of a divorce, yet his first wife and most of his children lived for years afterward.

Whatever the circumstances, one can only imagine the pain felt by all who went through that terrible time of war and reconstruction. Prime moved to Galveston, a seaport city renowned for gambling and immorality, and the new couple raised four more children. Young H.M. sprang from this second line, one that would not have existed if Prime had been faithful to his first wife. After World War I, young H.M.'s parents moved back to El Paso. Henry Senior went to work for his father in real estate. Speculations in properties led them to move several times over the next few years. They lived in a

Grandfather Robert Lee Morris, Mamie, and their children;
Henry Senior is to the right of Mamie.

series of small bungalows in El Paso near to family. Grandfather Hunter, the doctor, lived nearby, but his wife had separated from him and was living in Houston.

Grandfather Robert Lee Morris and his wife were also close by, and the Holy Spirit used this grandmother to bring the gospel message to young H.M. She was known as Mamie to the family, and she took a keen interest in the spiritual growth of her first grandson. As chief babysitter, she often spoke to him of the Lord and read the Bible to him. Years later, H.M. said this godly lady first introduced him to the grace of God and told him the way to salvation.

> Many people feel that little children have too much difficulty understanding about the Lord Jesus and His great salvation to be saved while they are small. Actually, as [Luke 18:16-17] indicates, it's really the other way around. It's the older people who find it difficult to understand about Christ and salvation, not the children! The Apostle Paul wrote to young Timothy: "From a child thou hast known the holy scriptures, which are able to make thee wise unto salvation through faith which is in Christ Jesus" (II Timothy 3:15). The word "child" (Greek brephos) actually can mean a very young child, or even an infant. As soon as a child can understand that there is a difference between right and wrong, he can be taught to understand that the Lord Jesus can forgive his sins and save him. The earlier in life he understands this, the more likely it is he will believe it.[1]

H.M. later wrote, "All I know is that I can never recall a time in my life when I did not know about the Lord Jesus and His love for me, and believe in Him. Mother also taught me about Christ, of course, as did my Sunday School teachers, but somehow I especially remember those talks with Grandmother."[2]

Grandmother "Mamie" Morris (left); John Robert and H.M. (right)

His special relationship with her is seen in a poem he wrote at the age of 11, during a particularly difficult time in his life. He presented it to his Grandmother Morris on Mother's Day soon after her husband passed away.

> The other day not long ago,
> When I came home to play,
> I learned that my dear Grandfather
> Had gone with God to stay.
>
> Granddad now is happy
> Because he is living above,
> But, ah, now he is gone away,
> I no longer share his love.

He is gone, but wait—
I still have the love of another,
One that I love, and one that loves me,
My patient and loving Grandmother.

She has God's light in her dear eye,
No one else can take her part,
Through all my cares and worries
She still remains deep in my heart.[3]

Christmas at Grandmother's house (left);
John Robert, H.M., and Richard Morris (right)

To her credit, his mother Ida insisted her son be raised in the church and made certain he was enrolled in Sunday school. She had two more sons in El Paso—John Robert Morris in 1921 and Richard "Dick" Stanley Morris in 1925—and she tried to raise them well. A prayer she pasted in the back of a baby book gives an insight into her mother's heart and foreshadows the role the Holy Spirit played in her life as she tended to the children God placed in her care. (See Appendix C.)

H.M., Richard, and John Robert

John Robert, H.M., and Richard (left); Morris
family at Ruidoso, New Mexico, in 1926 (right)

When H.M. was eight, his mother gave him a Bible of his
own. He began reading it, starting in Genesis, and about that
time began to be concerned about the Lord and shared the gospel enthusiastically with others. The indifference of friends was
often painful and frustrating. In later years, he wrote,

> The other kids considered me a sort of "goody-
> goody," and this was not a pleasant situation for an

introspective child such as I soon became. This was aggravated by the fact, after starting to school, that I nearly always was at the head of the class scholastically. A combination of moral rectitude and academic superiority tends to give one the position of "teacher's pet," and such a reputation, of course, is quite deadly, guaranteed to generate a high degree of peer-group unpopularity.[4]

Often alone, he became intensely interested in Western movies. El Paso was one of the wild frontier towns of the Old West, and the Western tradition was strong. His mother shared childhood stories of hiding on the roof to watch the battles of Pancho Villa in Juarez, just across the Rio Grande. Her father, as town doctor, waited until the shooting stopped and rushed down to tend the wounded.

It was still a rugged region of ranches, cowboys, and cavalrymen. The Unique Theater in town showed only cowboy movies, and young H.M. soon learned to identify with Tom Mix, Hoot Gibson, Buck Jones, Tom Tyler, and all the other glamorous cowboy stars of the silent films. Many years later, he told his family, "I acquired a large collection of 'penny-post-card' trading pictures of these stars and their exploits in celluloid, and one of my hardest decisions years later after finishing college, and after I had quit going to movies altogether,

Morris family

33

was to dispose of this collection."[5]

H.M. and his father were separated from his mother and brothers for several months during one childhood summer. Busy with work, his father gave him money every day to go to the movies. It might seem fun for a nine-year-old to run around old El Paso and hang around the cowboy theater, but a letter he wrote to his mother revealed disappointment in his father's promises and a longing for his family to be together. Loneliness was his steady companion even when he lived with his father.

In 1927, Henry Senior decided to move the family to booming Corpus Christi. They bought a lovely house on Atlantic Street, and armed with his new Bible, H.M. enthusiastically sought out friends to invite to Sunday school. His grandmother told him about the imminent return of Christ and assured him— evidently as a result of a visiting evangelist's calculation—that it could occur no later than 1933! There wasn't much time left, and he was eager to spread the news.

About that time, Billy Sunday came to Corpus Christi for revival meetings in a large warehouse on the other side of town. With great determination, H.M. managed to get there, alone, every day through a long series of bus rides. Years later, he told his own children how the children of Corpus Christi sat in one particular area

H.M. baptism, age 10

and Billy Sunday led them in verses of "Brighten the Corner Where You Are." It made a lasting impression on him. The light of God was beckoning, and even though his family life was not encouraging, H.M.'s tender heart responded.

Not long after, he realized he needed to be baptized and asked his parents to let him talk to the pastor. The pastor believed H.M. truly made the decision to follow Christ and, on his 10th birthday, baptized him at the First Baptist Church of Corpus Christie. Later in life, he said that these were the best and only happy times he could remember from his childhood.

3

The Refining Process

A s so often happens with young Christians, it wasn't long before H.M. encountered skeptics' arguments against the Bible. Friends visited his parents, and he overheard their questions: "Where did Cain get his wife?" and "How could Christ be born of a virgin?" These and others were asked but not answered that night. Still, simple faith helped H.M. to feel confident that there must be good answers somewhere.

Many events in H.M.'s life could have easily thwarted his spiritual growth and turned him toward a life of bitterness and defeat. He encountered an especially dark evil when his parents enrolled him in the Pioneer Club. The class was supposed to involve athletics and crafts. Tragically, the club meeting ended abruptly one night when parents of some of the older boys in the club discovered that the instructions included homosexual activities between the teacher and some students. The instructor was taken to jail, and H.M. was spared that horror.

Corpus Christi was a typical port city. Before Prohibition, the town included about 37 saloons, but by 1920 when Prohibition went into effect they were all dark and shuttered. However, the town was never "dry." The era ushered in bootleggers, smuggled hooch, and bathtub gin. It was not too surprising that Henry Senior kept a few cases of gin in the bathroom of their home. It was illegal, certainly, but more than that, the alcohol played a large role in the further fracturing of their family.

By 1929, the boom in Corpus Christi was over, and Henry Senior's real estate business began falling apart. The family was forced to rent out their home and move into a small, inexpensive cottage near the beach. Poverty, alcoholism, and business failure combined to destabilize the family, furthered by the looming devastation of the Great Depression.

That fall, H.M. registered for junior high school. The semester had barely begun when his brother John Robert became deathly ill with a ruptured appendix. Ida stayed day and night at the hospital, so H.M. and his younger brother Richard (Dick) were sent to Houston to stay with relatives. H.M. vigorously protested this decision because it meant separation from his family and going to junior high in an intense urban environment.

Nevertheless, the two boys were sent to live with Ida's sister Vivian and her husband Ernest, and this move proved to be permanent for H.M., who never returned to Corpus Christi. His younger brother was soon sent back to his mother, but H.M. stayed and transferred to Albert Sidney Johnston Junior High School in Houston's South End. He previously experienced two short sessions in Houston schools during primary grade years while vis-

H.M. and Muddy

iting his aunt and cousins. He remembered that there was quite a lot of boy-and-girl involvement in his cousins' school—and that was terrifying to one who was so introverted.

Ernest and Vivian were wealthy, and their home, with two socially active daughters, was often the site of Roaring Twenties-style parties with drinking and dancing. Fortunately, H.M.'s grandmother Amanda Hunter, affectionately known as Muddy, had moved there after her divorce to live with her daughter Vivian. Muddy lived in an apartment in Vivian's home, and H.M. now joined his grandmother in the apartment, essentially becoming part of this family for the next few years. The family had a somewhat religious background, but they were far more devoted to wealth and high society. However, Muddy, in spite of the disappointments in her life, faithfully attended the Baptist church with H.M. in tow.

Due to his introverted nature and, undoubtedly, the protection of the Holy Spirit, H.M. spent most of his time alone and avoided much of the negative influences surrounding him. Instead, he concentrated on academics and amusements of his own making. As a top student, he spent his spare time developing his interest in cowboy pictures and other movies. He concocted various scripts with plots, themes, and actors, and drew beautiful advertisement posters of his imaginary screenings. He never imagined that those scripts would be the precursor to hundreds of books and articles he later wrote for the encouragement and edification of believers all over the world.

Junior high school was difficult for an insecure and lonely child in 1930 for the same reasons that it is today. Nevertheless, his academic successes included awards in spelling bees, Latin, and sports writing. As a seventh grader, he participated in a citywide spelling bee that lasted for several months, first at

H.M. Morris

the local school, with the winners moving on to higher levels across the city. The contest was broadcast over the Houston radio waves with weekly events. Ultimately, he won the junior high division. This was the first of thousands of public speaking performances.

As an eighth grader, H.M. also became editor of the school's paper. The publication won a citywide contest, and he personally won awards as a sportswriter. An avid baseball fan, he listened faithfully to the broadcasts of the Houston Buffalos of the old Texas League and developed journalism skills writing for his school and even publishing in the Houston newspaper. He began to think seriously about a career in journalism, with hopes of becoming a sportswriter.

With his longtime passion for baseball, he became a member of the Knothole Gang, which allowed him to attend games with other children for a reduced admission. He invented a game similar to Fantasy Baseball with a full set of players and teams, complete with batting and pitching averages. Two gamers would draw "plays" out of a shoebox and proceed based on the averages. All of this calculating fostered a proficiency in mental arithmetic, which was useful many years later as he progressed in engineering. It also established his image as an oddball intellectual with no interest in normal junior high pursuits.

H.M. Morris

H.M.'s keen interest in baseball and writing skills were recognized when the local newspaper printed one of his poems, marking his first published work at age 15.

The Baseball News

I always read the daily news,
Consult the editorial views
(Although they seldom interest me)
And read the paper thoroughly;
But in the morn when I arise;
It's not in news my interest lies;
I'm not at ease til I survey
The baseball news of yesterday.

The trouble 'twixt Japan and China,
The Normandie, the great French liner,
The woes of Mexican Catholics,
Louisiana Politics,
Advertisements of movie passions,
The very latest Paris fashions,

All pass unheeded till I've seen

If Hubbell bested Dizzy Dean.

Plans to create a Utopia,
Threats of war in Ethiopia,
The choice of this week's French premier,
The ten best pictures of the year;
If Mrs. Astor gives a tea,
It very seldom interests me;
I much prefer to read about
How Lefty Grove struck Gehrig out.

A German treaty with Great Britain,
A feature story on a kitten,
Black widow spiders by the score,
The opening of a downtown store,
Bad blood between Japan and Russia,
Doesn't all of this disgust ya?
I'd rather know the player's name
Who knocked three homers in one game.

The arguments about the dole,
The criticisms of parole,
Balloons that reach beyond the air,
Murders happ'ning everywhere;
O leave all this is best, I've felt,
To Congress and to Roosevelt;
If I could have my way, I'd choose
A world of only baseball news.

The country was deep into the Great Depression, and in 1931 H.M.'s father, mother, and two younger brothers relocated to El Paso, while H.M. remained in Houston. In a short time, they returned to the Corpus Christi area, hoping to catch a break in the town of Ingleside, a small community where the Humble Oil Company planned to build a refinery. Finally, desperate and broke, the family moved to Houston and rented an apartment. Henry Senior left the family almost immediately. Ida tried to keep their marital problems from her sons, but it was obvious to all, even H.M., that the family was breaking up. He later recalled,

> I still remember the traumatic experience...of inadvertently overhearing a part of one of their last arguments, and hearing Dad snap back to Mother, "Well, I don't care whether you hate me or not!" I didn't stay to hear anymore, and that is one scene I wish I could forget altogether.[1]

H.M. later summed up his childhood and offered this insight:

> One of the primary needs of children is a sense of security and love. Probably the greatest threat to their security is the unrecognized fear that develops when they sense a tension between Mother and Dad. Their parents provide their guidance and sustenance and their protection, and all this becomes jeopardized when they begin to feel estrangement between them.
>
> Perhaps I sense this need more strongly than many people do because of these experiences of my own as a boy. Mother and Dad were separated, and later divorced, so that very little of my boyhood was spent in a normal home situation. From my 11th birthday on, I lived either with my grandmother in the home of my aunt and uncle, or with my mother and grandmother and two younger brothers. We had very little financial security, either, since this was during the depths of the great depression, and our family income was hard-earned and very minimal. Neverthe-

less, even though none of us knew much about the Lord in those days, we did know we were Christians and that somehow the Lord would see us through. He does, in fact, seem to have a special concern for those of his children who, through no fault of their own, have unusual family difficulties.[2]

For years, Ida earned a small amount of money by playing piano professionally for radio. She was known as The Piano Melody Maid and, within a few years, had a regular show with the professional name Yvonne Hunter. Even so, she was unable to support the family on her own. They could no longer afford an apartment, so she and her three boys moved in with Earnest and Vivian. However, this time there were four of them, and the only space available was an area in the attic that was roughly converted into two bedrooms. They lived there for a year—imagine a Houston attic in summer before air conditioning—and the experience added further drama to H.M.'s suffering social life. To his previous "reputation as an unsociable outsider was now added the epithet of an attic-dwelling pauper, and the 'in-crowd' at school made life generally miserable."[3] With life at home so

Ida as "Yvonne Hunter"

inhospitable, he devoted more and more time to his studies and tryouts for various sports, especially softball.

Believing it was best, Muddy and her brother John convinced Ida to file for divorce. The divorce papers were finalized in June 1932 with Henry Senior not even appearing for the proceedings.

Late that summer, the family went with Ernest and a large group of his business colleagues to a ranch for swimming, horseback riding, fishing, gambling, and conducting business deals. An unanticipated hurricane blew in, and the whole party spent the night in the supply room, the newest structure on the ranch. H.M. observed the panic and fear of death among others in the group but noticed that the Lord gave him real peace during the night. The next morning, they found most of the buildings on the ranch completely destroyed, but the supply room weathered the storm. Although just 14, he felt closer to the Lord than ever before and recognized his need for spiritual growth.

It wasn't long before things became even more unpleasant at his uncle and aunt's home. After a violent argument, Ernest told Ida and her family to leave and ordered that her sister, Vivian, was never to speak to her again. To H.M., this was traumatic, unexplained, and, in the midst of the Depression, catastrophic. However, he realized much later that it was providential, removing the young brothers from an increasingly destructive environment.

During those tumultuous years, Muddy was a stable guiding force in his life. She

H.M. at Aunt Kate's farm

45

consistently took him to church, advised him, and eased his loneliness by taking him on extended visits to see other family members. Muddy was from a large clan of pioneers descended from Reuben Hornsby, one of the original Texas colonists with Stephen F. Austin. Consequently, there were several family-owned ranches and farms to visit.

When asked years later about his grandmother, H.M. always said, "Yes, Muddy was quite a character." The photographs that exist today (circa 1900) show her to be the clown in the room. In fact, a set of photographs from the early days of her marriage display her quirky sense of humor. In one, she is dressed as a Confederate soldier. In another, she is lying on the floor seemingly shooting at intruders. Another has her rifling through her husband's pants pockets as he lies sleeping in his bed. A character, indeed!

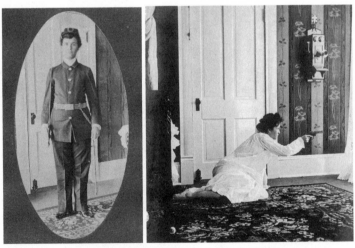

Muddy dressed as a soldier (left); Muddy playing cowboy (right)

Yet this grandmother, with her accumulated experiences from life in high society to the failure of her marriage, chose to leave her daughter's fine home where she lived and throw in her lot with the struggling Ida and three grandsons. Together, they rented a small apartment and worked to support the family. She played an increasing role in the growth and achievements of her grandson.

As a child in 1930, H.M. wrote a touching tribute to his grandmother.

H.M. and Muddy at La Jolla cave

"Muddy"

Her hair is gray, her legs are scarred,
From all she has done for me,
Her face is tired, her feet are sore,
And her hands are never free.

But she hardly complains of life's struggle,
And all the injustice within,
She goes through it all with a cheer,
And bravely battles with sin.

I'll always love and esteem her,
From a kid till I pass away,
But—wait the end is not over,
We'll be reunited some day.

She'll always be deep in my heart,
Although we're apart many miles,
I'll always remember her love,
The "Muddy" of wonderful smiles.

H.M. tried his hand at several jobs to make a contribution to the family budget. In Corpus Christi, he made a short attempt at being a "newsie" selling papers, but the competition was a tough crowd of older boys. Later in Houston, he sold magazines door to door and delivered a weekly shopping paper. At 14, when finances were desperate, he managed to land a job as a bag boy at the market, earning $1.50 for 14 hours of work. That arrangement ended with the New Deal under Roosevelt that prohibited the employment of boys and girls under 16.

His entrance into San Jacinto High in 1932 brought new challenges. Like all teenagers, H.M. felt a strong desire to fit in and tried out for various sports. In spite of his interest and desire to participate, he could never quite make the team.

Without money and transportation of any kind, he was unable to join in most school activities, including dating. He couldn't afford to attend any professional baseball or football games and was too old for the Knothole Gang discounts. However, there was still adventure for the brave and impoverished! He told his children much later,

> A common risk sport in those days was to try to get in to the Rice Institute football games, either by climbing the fence or by hiding in the stands ahead of time. I succeeded at the latter several times. It never occurred to me at the time that there were any moral aspects to such an undertaking—it was merely a challenge to overcome if you were good enough.[4]

His mother, an accomplished musician, was determined to help her son develop socially. So, she taught him to dance. The newly acquired rhythm gave H.M. a little more confidence and a bit more success at making friends with girls.

Three brothers in 1935 (left); graduation from San Jacinto High in 1935 (right)

A family friend, the husband of H.M.'s English teacher, also endeavored to help the brilliant but underprivileged teen by teaching him to drive. Though it was an ancient car, it served the purpose. A great uncle got H.M. a job at the Texaco gas station working as a "pump monkey." Barely able to drive, and having never owned a car or acquired any knowledge of mechanics, he managed to bluff his way through, learning the routine chores of pumping gas and checking oil.

With a little money, transportation, and improved social skills, H.M. was able to get a date for the senior prom with a classmate named Mary Bethany, with whom he fell madly in love. The relationship went nowhere, but, curiously, it was Mary Bethany that God used to steer this young scholar in a life-altering direction. He had determined to pursue journalism at the University of Texas in Austin, but Mary Bethany enrolled in Rice Institute, which had no journalism program. Suddenly, journalism wasn't so important.

4

The Fires of Temptation

Rice Institute (now Rice University) turned out to be an ideal choice. Although he chose it because of Mary Bethany, the school had an excellent record for preparing graduates to acquire good jobs. In 1935, the pall of the Depression remained and good-paying jobs were scarce. Yet, Rice engineering graduates fared well. H.M.'s family was still very poor, so the chance of a profitable future in engineering attracted him.

Rice Institute

More importantly, Rice was a privately endowed school that charged no tuition. It had a high academic reputation—many called it the Harvard of the South—and admission was difficult to get. Fortunately, H.M.'s grade point average was just good enough to qualify. Without this tuition-free advantage, he probably couldn't have finished college.

Rice offered majors in only four branches of engineering. With no mechanical, electrical, or chemical experience, H.M. elected to enter the fourth branch—civil engineering. He enjoyed physics and trigonometry in high school and thought that civil engineering might correlate with those interests.

Rice required all students to live in the dorms during their freshman year, which included "continually being forced into a wide variety of embarrassing and uncomfortable activities"[1] excused as hazing. However, Muddy just happened to know the Rice bursar personally. Muddy invited the bursar to the house one Sunday afternoon and persuaded him to admit H.M. and make an exception that allowed H.M. to remain at home. This seemingly small decision protected him from the often debasing influences of secular dorm life.

Rice Institute

There were no welfare payments, food stamps, or government assistance in those days. Ida and Muddy could work, but the two younger boys were in school. It took the combined incomes of H.M. and the two women to keep the family afloat. His grandmother received a small wage working at a flower shop, while his mother made a meager income at a variety of secretarial jobs and as a pianist on radio stations. H.M. worked at three different gas stations during the summer and fall of that freshman year.

> We lived in a small apartment about halfway between the Rice campus and the downtown area where I worked, roughly three miles from each. With no car, I had to walk to and from both school and work. Walking home late each night after the filling station closed meant I had to walk through one of Houston's main street-walker areas. I managed to decline all solicitation, partly because of moral convictions, but I suppose partly also because of financial considerations and general timidity. Whatever the reason, I have thanked the Lord many times since that, unlike most young men of my acquaintance, I somehow was restrained from all premarital sexual experiences.[2]

Surrounded by mechanics whom he described as "moral lechers" in a letter to his brother, vile language, and a business owner who "only occasionally" committed adultery, H.M. received quite an education about the world as a 17-year-old.

Soon the purchase of a car became a priority. Muddy was able to make the down payment, and with H.M. determined to handle the monthly payments, they purchased the cheapest car they could find: a 1929 Ford Model A two-door. The affectionately named "Belinda" was a source of pride and joy to the family. It would grind its way back and forth for them for the next three years. One of the only times in H.M.'s life that he could ever remember being "fighting mad" was when another driver fell asleep at the wheel and slammed into his beloved Belinda's left front door. Poor Belinda didn't last long but made an important contribution to his college success.

H.M. quickly discovered that college was vastly different from high school. The assignments were long and hard, and he soon fell behind because he was working nights at the gas station. About to fail chemistry and unable to keep up in engineering drawing, he was in real danger of flunking out of school. There was no other choice but to quit his job and devote his evenings to schoolwork. Fortunately, he was able to pull up his grades and made the honor roll by the end of the year.

However, the family's financial situation demanded that he produce an income. H.M. made the National Youth Administration roll, one of the New Deal agencies, which paid students 25 cents per hour to work around the campus. He was assigned to the civil engineering laboratories, which provided valuable experience and familiarization with the testing machines and lab equipment.

After his almost-calamitous first semester, H.M. maintained a very high grade point average. As a result he qualified for a yearly scholarship and was eventually elected to three honor societies: Tau Beta Pi (honorary engineering fraternity), Sigma Xi (honorary scientific research society), and Phi Beta Kappa (honorary science society).

In one sense, he was an unlikely candidate for an engineering career. His mechanical aptitude, as he claimed, was "almost nonexistent," with the exception of what little he acquired working at the gas station. However, he excelled at mathematics and theoretical science, skills necessary in engineering. He figured out how to cope with most mechanical situations and became "a good draftsman and surveyor, which were mechanical skills of a sort."[3]

As H.M. progressed through the semesters, he became more involved in the social scene and campus activities. Though Rice students were supposedly the intellectual elite, many of them still shared the typical college preoccupation with dating, drinking, dancing, and smoking. He tried to fit in, but his participation in extracurricular social activities was minimal. When he later reflected on that time, H.M. believed the Holy Spirit kept him from getting involved in many of the temptations that surrounded him. He played on the Engineers' Club intramural basketball team and the Baptist church's softball team, but he admitted, "As an athlete, I was unexciting."[4]

H.M. Morris

His spiritual activities and interests continued somewhat as he attended church and Sunday school at a large Southern Baptist church. However, he had stopped reading the Bible and gained little spiritual growth by his association with the church.

Although determined to study engineering, H.M. still loved writing. He continued to write poetry, publishing a few humorous ones in the school publications. He even made a few efforts at writing religious poetry. In fact, he wrote and published a dark poem, called "The Godless Souls," in response to his classmates' atheism. It is a strangely foreshadowing poem about the futile efforts of godless men to find meaning in life. Written in a period of H.M.'s life when his personal relationship with God was probably at its most dim, the need to address the empty "wisdom" of the humanists compelled him to write his perspective of atheism.

The Godless Souls
by Henry Morris, October 1936

A canyon stretches, grim and dank,
And there, in ghastly, silent rank
Are men that grope in single file,
Each from each one a thousand mile.
A canyon stretches past the sight,
Nor turns its way to left nor right,
Upon the sides a massive block
That strains its hulking vastness high
To reach, to pierce, and pass the sky;
And through it all, the leaden air
Rolls fiercely, hotly, everywhere,
And beats the wall with sullen roar
As though it sought an exit-door,
But failing, struggles frantically
To crash and crush the rock, and flee
In panic-taken, maddened charge
The creatures bound within the gorge.

How slowly they drudge
In the mire-soggen mulch,
And push through the sludge

Of a Godless Gulch.
How weakly they cower
And sink in the sands;
How bleakly the Tower
Of Nothingness stands.

More silent than the desert's tombs,
A distant tower-image looms,
A shadow; yet the creatures plod
And consecrate a shadow-god,
Whose temple is a shadow-shrine,
A tower, where fools would entwine
Their Godless Souls in emptiness,
Where fools seek cosmic loneliness.
And onward yet, on, on they grope,
Their beings reft of mortal hope,
Their souls spliced taut in mortal strands
That mock the strain of bleeding hands
To part, the palsied souls' distress
To interweave in nothingness.
They'll struggle on, but they'll not reach
The tower; finally, falling, each
Shall from a godless world rebel
And long the agonies of hell.

So slowly they drudge
In the bog-rotted mulch,
In the deepening sludge
Of a Godless Gulch.
How long is the wait
From a Godless goal;
How bleak is the fate
Of a Godless Soul.

H.M. encountered evolutionary indoctrination from the beginning of his college experience. "The notorious Julian Huxley, grandson of evolutionist Thomas Huxley, had been the founder of [Rice's] biology department, and his atheistic tone was still strongly characteristic of the department when I was there. Huxley was probably the leading evolutionist of the 20th century." Although engineering courses were mostly

Family on graduation day

quantitative and factual, the literature selections in the English courses were "definitely slanted against Christianity, and there were many humanistic overtones in the physics and chemistry courses."[5]

H.M. was vaguely aware that the college community was generally evolutionist as well as non-Christian, but he was far too occupied with studies and working to be concerned about such matters. He later wrote that he remembered "skimming through a book I found in the library, entitled *I Believe in God and Evolution*, by a medical man, Dr. Keen. I thought then that would solve whatever problem there might be along these lines, and thenceforth became a nominal evolutionist as well as a nominal Christian."[6]

Becoming a civil engineer not only involved long hours of study but also various summer jobs with the Texas Highway Department. He found work first as surveyor for an underpass construction project, then as a surveyor, draftsman, and com-

Professor H.M. Morris (far right) and survey class

puter on a crew supervising the construction of miles of high embankments and several bridges. This was valuable field experience for a future civil engineer and even involved learning to walk along bridge girders high in the air while cradling a surveying instrument on one shoulder.

Those few years of H.M.'s life in the university were some of the hardest he had yet faced. The physical demands of working, the enormous academic load, and the effects of secular campus life were almost overwhelming.

H.M. Morris

5

Grace and Peace Multiplied

H.M. was in his junior year at Rice Institute with an engineering career on the horizon when he realized his next logical step was to find a wife. He intended to address this issue sooner rather than later. Logic was his strong suit, and he determined to take this step based on that concept, especially in view of the fact that he was unskilled in romantic pursuits. He occasionally dated in college but did not find anyone he considered suitable for his image of a wife and future mother. He had personally witnessed the results of a hasty marriage and the devastation of a failed one.

True to his logical instincts, H.M. made a list of eligible young women whom he had never dated and who seemed to meet the qualifications. Then, holding a pencil above the paper, he closed his eyes and let it fall, spurning logic and trusting fate. The point fell on a childhood classmate from junior high named Mary Louise Beach.

> I did not seek the Lord's will in this action at all—such a thing never occurred to me—but He was guiding anyway. Though we didn't know it, He had a purpose to be accomplished in us, and He brought us together in this rather unlikely way. The Bible says:

"Whoso findeth a wife findeth a good thing" (Proverbs 18:22). The greatest discovery of my life was when I "found" Mary Louise![1]

H.M. had no reason to think she would remember him. They attended the same junior high and high school, but she was outgoing and popular, so predictably their paths rarely crossed. Although they were in the same grade, he was 17 months younger, having skipped grades in elementary school.

Mary Louise Beach in sixth grade

In March 1938, H.M. got up the nerve to ask Mary Louise for a date. That first call was almost the last—she wasn't home, and her father answered the phone. Mr. Beach, an electrician, was previously injured by a severe electrical shock and fall from a telephone pole. As a result, his speech was impaired, and over the phone H.M. thought he was drunk. Familiar as he was with the damage an alcoholic father brings

Mary Louise

to a family, he considered removing Mary Louise from the eligibility list. However, he tried again a week or two later, and once again the father answered. H.M. almost hung up but somehow managed to ask for Mary Louise. He remarked many years later to his own children, "On what slender threads are important events suspended!"[2]

David Morey Beach and Louise Mary Schuller

Mary Louise was the daughter of David Morey Beach and Louise Mary Schuller, both from large pioneering Texas families. The Beaches originally came from England with the Puritans to New Haven, Connecticut, in 1638. Beach descendants progressed west, through Pennsylvania, Ohio, and finally to Texas. The Schullers emigrated from Germany in 1848 and settled in the Houston area.

Mary Louise was the youngest of four, two brothers and two sisters. Led by a staunch German mother, the family attended a Lutheran church (one of the early pio-

The Beach Family

neer churches in Texas) that merged with the Evangelical and Reformed denomination. Because of the large German population in Houston, services at the church were held in both German and English. Mary Louise became a Christian at age 15, enrolled as a member, and taught a Sunday school class, although her knowledge of the Bible was minimal.

She could not enroll in college because her family was far from affluent and her grades were not high enough to apply to tuition-free Rice Institute. Her father worked as an electrician during the time when horse-drawn trolleys were being converted to electricity. Although he had done well, the Depression brought hard times, and he lost his job after his accident. As a result, Mary Louise went to work after high school. She held various jobs as a sales clerk, receptionist, and an assistant in a doctor's office.

The telephone call from H.M. came as a complete surprise. It took her several moments to remember the name, and she wondered how it happened that he would call her for a date. It was nearly a year before she knew about the list.

She agreed to go out, and on their first date he took her to see *Snow White and the Seven Dwarfs*. They were an awkward duo; he was quiet and serious, while she was a self-described chatterbox. It took a year of off-and-on dating before Mary Louise was ready to give up other suitors, but by H.M.'s senior year she decided to spend time with him exclusively.

Shortly after their first date, Mary Louise and her cousin, not understanding the danger, visited a fortune-teller just for fun. Mary Louise was shocked when the woman described H.M. as her new boyfriend and as the one she would eventually marry. Furthermore, the woman told her that he would soon give Mary Louise an expensive present. On Mary Louise's birthday soon after, H.M. gave her a nice suitcase to use on a trip to a summer Leadership Training School she was planning to attend. He recalled later:

> Just how the presumably demonic spirits who supplied this fortune-teller with such information were able to anticipate such coming events, or why they were interested enough to do so, I don't know. In any case, when Mary Louise told me these things months later, both of us realized that phenomena of this sort were dangerous and were off-limits to Christians. Rather than attracting us to the occult, as perhaps the spirits had intended, it repelled us, and we have both stayed very clear of such things ever since.[3]

As their relationship deepened and they began to face thoughts of marriage, their love for each other grew stronger, and so did their concern for the Lord. They knew their first responsibility was to Christ, and they engaged in many serious talks about the future and spiritual responsibilities. Both attended church regularly, but neither was receiving much spiritual food or doing any significant Bible study.

One night on the front porch of her home, H.M. proposed, and they discussed their future life together. He said,

> We had prayer together for the first time, asking God to bless our home and children, helping us to be faithful in serving Him through our union. We didn't know much about such things, but the Lord certainly has answered this prayer, far beyond what we could have dreamed at the time.[4]

Although committed to each other, an official engagement had to wait. H.M. graduated from Rice in June 1939, but the country was still recovering from the Great Depression, and jobs proved hard to find. Only a few companies were interviewing Rice engineering graduates for employment. He finally accepted a position with the Texas Highway Department with the "less-than-imposing title of 'Junior Office Assistant,' and the still less impressive salary of $120 per month. Most of the other engineering graduates in my class didn't fare even this well."[5]

Finally, in October he received notice that he was rated at the top

John Robert, Ida, and H.M. at Rice graduation

Mary Louise at H.M.'s graduation (left); Mary Louise and H.M. in 1939 (right)

of the Civil Service examination and was approved as a potential Junior Engineer in the U.S. Civil Service with a salary scale beginning at $2,000 per year. Marriage was now a possibility!

Two days later, a telegram arrived offering a position as Junior Engineer with the International Boundary Commission in El Paso, Texas, to begin almost immediately on October 23. Wasting no time, H.M. purchased an engagement ring and presented it to Mary Louise on October 10, 1939. It didn't fit, but she wore it anyway all through the going-away dinner party she threw in his honor.

H.M. started out on the long drive to El Paso with the promise to Mary Louise that they would marry as soon as he could accumulate leave time and save enough money for minimum expenses.

As before, a grandparent came to his aid. Dr. John Hunter, his maternal grandfather, still lived in El Paso and provided a place to stay, enabling H.M. to save the necessary money.

In September 1939, the year H.M. began work in El Paso, Dr. Hunter suffered a severe illness. He and Muddy had been divorced for over 20 years, yet she still loved him and immediately left Houston to take care of him. With H.M. arriving in October, she had sufficient reason to stay in El Paso and continue her influence over her grandson while caring for her invalid husband.

Muddy continually made enormous differences in H.M.'s life. She served as his stable and nourishing counselor. He actually spent more time with her than with his own mother. She took him in when he was a confused and lonely junior higher, separated from his family. She took him on extended vacations, encouraged him, and made sure he attended church.

She sacrificed financially for him, got him into college, provided the down payment for a car, bought his college ring, paid his dues, and even co-signed for Mary Louise's engagement ring.

Muddy at home

Through those years, life was not easy for her. Her marriage had ended in divorce and her two daughters were estranged from each other. In 1937, she was run over by a car, a terrible accident that broke her legs and injured her back. Yet, she continued to support herself and others.

The day after Thanksgiving, Muddy caught a cold. The illness worsened, and she was eventually diagnosed with lymphatic leukemia, an untreatable condition. Dr. Hunter was with her every day until she slipped away to heaven on January 8, 1940.

For H.M., the sadness and loneliness turned into "cold feet" about his upcoming marriage, and he suggested a postponement. However, Muddy had loved Mary Louise and had urged him not to let her condition affect their plans. Once again, God used her self-sacrifice—even in her last days—to further His plans for H.M.

In El Paso, the desire for spiritual growth began to take root in H.M.'s heart. The first Sunday H.M. was in El Paso, he visited the First Baptist Church, the same one he attended as a child. This solid, Bible-based church eventually proved to be a blessing and a stabilizing influence, but on this particular Sunday it almost brought disastrous consequences, prompting him to consider abandoning church altogether. That evening he wrote to Mary Louise:

> At the preaching service, a converted Jew was preaching—in fact, holding a revival. It rather rubbed me the wrong way how they had advertised this fact in a somewhat sensational manner, but I went anyway. He preached for a while about sin and hell, then started the invitation and really used every possible means of embarrassing and shaming everyone there into joining the church. Not content with exhorting those who had never been saved and baptized, he began working on those whose church membership was elsewhere, and who, consequently, were backsliders, and ashamed of their religion, etc., into which category I seemed to fall. Finally, he had everyone else stand, proclaiming that all who stood but were not members of a church where they lived were thereby lying, and entreating those remaining seated to summon what decency remained in them and unite with the church. I was seated, of course, and before long, several kind souls began coming up, one at a time, putting their arms around me, and generally putting me on a very disconcerting spot. Pretty soon, even the preacher came down to plead with me. Boy, was I glad to get out of there! I've been mad and upset about that all afternoon.[6]

After visiting several other churches, H.M. returned to First Baptist because it was the most biblical in its teaching. A childhood friend persuaded him to attend the Baptist Training

Union young adult meeting and get involved with the Friendship Circle youth gatherings. He observed a warmth and depth in these people and an interest in the Bible he had not encountered in Houston.

> I soon began to read the Bible again myself. I had been far away from the Lord during high school and college days, even though regular in attendance at Sunday School and church and generally believed by others to be quite religious. Since I was no longer dating nearly every night, or studying, I had some spare time, and so started reading Scripture again, more than I ever had since the months soon after

Mary Louise on her wedding day

receiving a Bible as a small boy.[7]

H.M. began to love the Word of God, not only in theory but in reality. He still had some unresolved questions. Neither did he know how to reconcile the Genesis account of creation with science. Nevertheless, the Holy Spirit guided him, and he soon accepted the fact that the Bible is truth and that, even though he could not find the answers, they must be there. Quietly and persistently, the Holy Spirit nourished a lifelong commitment to apologetics, the logical and scientific defense of the Bible.

As soon as H.M. got a week off from work, he headed back to Houston. On January 24, 1940, Mary Louise and H.M. married, surrounded by family and friends, with a beautiful ceremony at the First Evangelical Lutheran Church in Houston. A few weeks later, he expressed his love in a Valentine's Day poem.

When I consider all the little things
Of everyday that make you dear, I see
A myriad of precious hours; a memory
Of loving you that only loving brings.
I love you now, and in the days to be
My deepest heart a silent carol sings;
And I'll have wealth beyond the dreams of Kings,
Because I know you'll share that love with me.
Then, one day, when the paean of heaven rings,
We'll meet our Lord together. Surely He
Will bless our love for all eternity,
For love, like hope, in men eternal springs.
Yet though I, for a love unending, pray,
I could not love you more, dear, than today

February 14, 1940

For H.M., it seemed that things were coming together—a steady job, a bright future, and now a treasured partner to stand beside him to provide comfort and support for the rest of his life. He would surely describe this time as "grace and peace multiplied" (1 Peter 1:2).

6

A Student in the Desert

For an aspiring engineer, H.M.'s earlier work in Houston with the Texas Highway Department was demanding and technical. It included drafting and specifications on various highway structures such as culverts and underpasses. However, in El Paso the work took on the much more challenging aspects of professional investigation, analysis, and design.

He became largely responsible for the preliminary studies, final designs, plans, and estimates for 11 Rio Grande River bridges. His other structural designs included preliminary rough plans for dams on the Rio Grande and Devil's Rivers, hydraulic structures such as flumes, canals, gauging stations, and small buildings.

Under the supervision of two highly qualified

H.M. at the Boundary Commissions office

73

hydraulic engineers, H.M. conducted numerous studies, such as backwater curves and hydraulic design of canals, gates, and desilting basins. The main project involved analysis of the effect that various dams would have on the flow of the Rio Grande and its tributaries. During this project, H.M. developed a number of new and effective computational techniques. By the end of the study, he had written an extensive technical study titled *Report on the Rio Grande Water Conservation Investigation*, co-authored by his supervisor, who wrote the introduction and administrative analysis. This book eventually served as the planning base for the dams and control systems that were built on the Rio Grande in later years and was the basis for his promotion to full membership in the scientific honor society Sigma Xi.

Mary Louise and H.M.

From highways to waterways, H.M. made great strides in professional knowledge and practice. He developed a fascination and expertise in the many processes associated with water. Though he was unaware of it, H.M. was being uniquely prepared for the tasks and opportunities that would come.

Like any young newly married couple, he and Mary Louise went through many adjustments and changes. Making ends meet is difficult during the best of economic times, but the U.S. was still deep in the Great Depression. He wrote many years later:

Although my salary was small, even by 1940 standards ($2000 per year!), we felt we could get by on it and there was no need for her to look for a job. In those days, in fact, it was generally considered that a husband who couldn't support his wife on his own salary had no business getting married at all....Our clothing and household budgets had to be minimal. She had to be very frugal in her buying and ingenious at sundry devices for dollar-stretching. Only in later years were we able to afford such appliances as a refrigerator and washing machine, much later a clothes drier [sic] and dishwasher.[1]

We moved quite a lot in those few years, living first in an apartment a block from Big Daddy [Dr. Hunter]. Then in a wonderful little one-bedroom house in northeast El Paso, then in an apartment down near the First Baptist Church, then an apartment within walking distance of downtown, and finally in a duplex not far from our first apartment. Usually our moves were occasioned by rent increases which we felt we couldn't afford.[2]

Though still immature in the faith, they decided their home would be a Christian one, and one of their first decisions was the choice of a church. H.M. considered himself a Baptist, but Mary Louise was a Lutheran, so they decided to attend a Methodist or Presbyterian church.

However, it did not take many weeks to find that the one they really enjoyed was the First Baptist Church. "The pastor was Dr. I. L. Yearby, a fundamental, pre-millennial Bible-believing Southern Baptist who really preached the Word with clarity and power."[3] Neither of them had ever heard such preaching, and the power of the Word of God began to have an impact.

Not long after they began attending, Dr. Yearby preached a series on the book of Revelation and "for the first time the blessed hope of the Lord's imminent coming" was impressed upon them.[4] For over 60 years, H.M. kept a plaque on his office wall that read "Perhaps Today," expecting Christ's return momentarily. This phrase had a lifelong influence on his ministry, focusing his activities toward evangelism.

The young people at First Baptist, both married and single, welcomed them and quickly involved them in Bible classes and the Baptist Training Union. It wasn't long before Mary Louise decided to be baptized, and as they became more knowledgeable in the Word, each got involved in teaching a Sunday school class for junior high students.

From time to time, the First Baptist Church sponsored excellent guest speakers that contributed to their spiritual growth. One speaker made a particularly strong impression. Dr. Irwin Moon brought his "Sermons from Science" lectures to the El Paso Auditorium in 1941. He gave a lecture on the significance of the great Flood—complete with a discussion of the possible effects of a Venus-like atmospheric canopy that might maintain the pre-Flood climate and allow for the long lifespans recorded in Genesis. H.M. had never heard anything like this before, and it stimulated an interest that remained with him for the rest of his life. Dr. Moon's messages generated a confidence in the absolute authority and scientific accuracy of the Bible—a conviction he had not known before.

Immersed in sound teaching, influenced by Christian friends, and involved in opportunities for service, H.M. flourished in his relationship with the Lord, as did Mary Louise.

The social life at the International Boundary Commission revolved primarily around its softball team. The commission's team was in a league composed of teams from various governmental agencies such as the Post Office and Border Control. Always a baseball enthusiast, H.M. joined the Boundary Commission team and later recounted to his children:

> I played either third base or pitcher, and was good enough to play on the all-star team one year. Once I even hit two home runs in one game! My main weakness was high pop flies—not hitting them, but catching them. The only black eye I ever received was from a hard grounder down the third base line that took an unexpected hop eyeward instead of gloveward.
>
> All of our games were "hard pitch," rather than the popular "soft-pitch" style. I got to be a fairly good pitcher, at least in our own league, though never comparable in speed to the really good softball pitchers. The games were good fun and exercise, however, and the wives enjoyed the fellowship in the stands.[5]

Certainly the biggest adjustment for H.M. and Mary Louise was the arrival of their first son. Prior to his birth in May 1942, H.M., although very successful in his job, had not received a raise, and their budget was very tight. Later, H.M. recalled:

> It was late in 1941 when Mary Louise first announced we were going to have a baby. I had been working as a junior engineer with the federal government at a

salary of only $167 per month. This was a civil service job, and in those days, the only way a raise could be obtained in such a position was by an offer for a promotion from some other federal agency. We were barely getting by and there seemed no way we could possibly afford the coming medical and hospital bills on my salary. We had recently started our daily devotional periods and that morning I felt constrained to pray earnestly for the Lord somehow to meet this financial need. As we were praying, the doorbell rang. It was a messenger boy with a telegram offering a job with another federal agency in another state at the next higher rank at a $50 monthly raise. With this competitive offer, my own agency was able to give me the same promotion, effective immediately, and the extra income saved for several months was, indeed, just sufficient to pay all the bills when our son was born.[6]

They named their son Henry Madison Morris III. In a letter to his mother, H.M. wrote an overwhelmed and proud response, "Gee, he sure is something! I've never had such a feeling before, and it's pretty good. Sure wish all of you could see him."[7] The bill for eight days in the hospital was $54.25, and the doctor bill was $65.

H.M. and Henry III in May 1942

HM Jr., HM Sr., HM III, Dick, Bobby

About this time, a group of men at First Baptist introduced H.M. to the Gideons, an organization dedicated to making the Word of God available to every person in every nation. H.M. was so impressed with these godly individuals that he joined the organization, saying it was "one of the finest groups of men I've ever known. I hope and pray that I can come up to their standards and do my part of the work, whatever it is."[8] These men soon included him as they met on Saturdays for lunch, Scripture reading, and prayer. He wrote in a letter, "You just can't imagine the blessings and inspiration we get out of those meetings. I wouldn't take anything for them."

July 1942

These older champions of the Word became mentors to this young professional, and he soon became deeply involved in the ministry of distributing the Bible. He was most enthused about raising money to purchase 10,000 New Testaments to hand out to soldiers ready to ship out to Europe for the war effort. By April of that year, he could be found down at the train depot every Monday night handing out New Testaments to soldiers passing through.

7

For Love of Country

When H.M. and Mary Louise married, Europe was fighting World War II. The U.S. military was not drafting married men, and H.M. assumed that, with his degree and a government job, there was very little chance he would need to consider a military option.

However, when Pearl Harbor was attacked on December 7, 1941, they suspected their home life would be dramatically affected by the crisis. Mary Louise was four months pregnant with their first child. As the U.S. prepared for war, the military draft extended to fathers unless they were in war-essential occupations.

Rather than be drafted as privates in the Army, several engineers at the Boundary Commission decided to apply for commissions as ensigns in the Civil Engineering Corps of the Navy. There, in the Seabees, they could maximize their engineering training.

H.M. applied with the Navy, and they considered him to be "professionally and educationally qualified for the appointment as Ensign Class CEC-V(S)."[1] In May 1942, he reported to Dallas for an interview, with induction to follow. As with many men of his generation, duty to country superseded private concern for family or career.

With their infant son in tow, the couple headed for Houston for a last visit with family before driving on to Dallas where H.M. would enter military service. It was a melancholy trip, with the pending separation and the hardships of war weighing heavily on their hearts.

During his time as a student at Rice, H.M. was greatly influenced by an engineering professor named L.B. Ryon. Professor Ryon had followed H.M.'s progress in El Paso and wrote a recommendation for him that was included in his application for the Navy:

> I have known Mr. Morris for seven years. He was graduated from this institution in June 1939 with a B.S. in C.E. degree. He was in my classes for two years. He was one of the best men we have had: an excellent student, clear and original thinker, and had a fine personality....I have kept close watch on Mr. Morris and think he has done well.
>
> It is my pleasure to highly recommend Mr. Morris as a young engineer of ability and promise, of high moral character, of sound physique, and of excellent personal characteristics. I believe he is fine officer material.
>
> L.B. Ryon, Professor of Civil Engineering.

When Professor Ryon realized H.M. was visiting in Houston, he asked him to come to Rice. To H.M.'s amazement, Ryon offered him a position as Instructor in Civil Engineering. The school was designated as a training center for Naval ROTC and Navy V-12 students, and Professor Ryon was able to persuade the Navy commandant at Rice to have H.M.'s appointment in the Seabees deferred indefinitely on the grounds that he would be much more valuable to the war effort in a teaching capacity. H.M. was ordered by the commander in New Orleans to take the position and serve as a Navy instructor while retaining civilian status. He would teach the necessary engineering skills to scores of cadets who were training to be officers.

This was a daunting assignment for one so young. H.M. was just beginning his work as an engineer. The thought of graduate school or a teaching career had not entered his mind. All the professors at Rice were mature and held advanced degrees. He, on the other hand, had never even made a lesson plan or taught a class. But the salary was considerably higher than at the Boundary Commission, and he could stay with his wife and child. Just 23 years old and quite apprehensive, he accepted the position.

H.M., Mary Louise, and Henry III in 1942

As a teacher at Rice, H.M. was in "essential status" and subject to deferment from induction into the Armed Forces. However, the war intensified, and in April 1944 the Navy Department changed policy. It no longer allowed the deferment of men age 26 or under for the purpose of instruction in the Navy College Program. The commanding officer at Rice had no alternative but to release him from his current duty. Once again, H.M. applied for a commission in the U.S. Naval Reserve, eager to do his duty and ready to assume his share of the danger that most young men of his generation faced.

But by this time, the intense study and teaching schedule had taken its toll, and his eyesight had suffered. The Navy declined his application for officer, but he was still eligible to be drafted as a private. However, his draft number never came up, and he remained an instructor at Rice.

John Robert Morris (left); H.M. and Richard "Dick" Morris (right)

During these years, few families escaped the devastating effects of the war. The Morris family was no exception. Unable to afford college and anxious to serve their country, H.M.'s younger brothers, John Robert and Dick, both enlisted. Dick joined the Navy. He shipped off to the South Pacific for much of the war. John Robert trained as an Air Force pilot at San Antonio Aviation Cadet Center, and then received his wings in Lubbock.

In the spring of 1944, John Robert was sent overseas to India and assigned to fly a C-47 cargo plane over the famous Burma Hump with supplies for the U.S.'s Chinese allies. On one of these missions, his plane came under fire, and he was killed on August 9, 1944, at the age of 23.

On that particular day, John Robert was substituting as a navigator for a sick buddy. The exact

John Robert Morris

details were never revealed, but reportedly the plane was shot down and crashed high up the slope on the Hump. Several weeks later, H.M.'s mother, Ida Morris, received a War Department telegram informing her that John Robert was missing in action. Like many in her situation, she continued writing letters and hoping for a positive report.

Bobby darling:

Well, well, well, so you've done gone and got yourself "missing in action." I'm completely and thoroughly disgusted with you....Received a little love letter from the Adjutant General yesterday afternoon, you know, "The Secretary of War desires me to express his deep regret that your son, Second Lieutenant John Robert Morris has been reported missing in action since nine August in Asiatic Theater. If further details or other information are received you will be promptly notified." If you wanted so much to get your picture put in the papers, why didn't you just say so, and I'd have managed it, didn't need to go to all that trouble to get it in....

I promised you I wouldn't worry if I got one of these little love letters, that is, not until they sent your dog tags home to me, and honey, I'm not about to break my promise to you. Of course, I'll admit my stomach did a couple of flip-flops as I read the message, and I still have a sort of empty, vacuum sort of feeling, and just a little "woozy" in the head, but after the first little shock of finding out that you're not a "big boy" after all and get lost when you get away from home, wears off, I'll be OK.

Lieutenant John Robert and mother Ida

They had special prayers for you at prayer meeting last night....And, honey, even though we don't know where you are, I know God does, and if you are still alive, I know He will give you and the other boys with you the physical strength to go through whatever pain, anguish, torture, etc., you may have already had and still have to face, and the spiritual comfort and faith He always gives if we only ask for it. If you weren't a Christian, and I weren't a Christian, I would probably have a complete breakdown, but at times like these, we really learn what is meant by "the peace that passeth all understanding"—don't we?

Lots and lots of love, as ever, Mother

Many weeks passed (and many more letters were written) before Ida received the final news that John Robert's body had been recovered.

For H.M., there was some comfort in knowing that his brother had grown in his relationship with the Lord in recent years. In fact, he had unofficially taken on the role of chaplain in his unit. John Robert had written H.M. and

John Robert and Ida

requested several boxes of Gideon New Testaments to give to his buddies. Through his testimony, several became followers of Christ—some even after his death.

8

Constrained by the Love of Christ

H.M., Mary Louise, and their infant son moved in with her family in Houston. After a brief period, they secured an apartment near the campus. Classes started in September 1942, and H.M. was quickly immersed in the responsibilities of a college professor. He admitted later:

> The first couple of days there were all but disastrous. I was assigned a large class in surveying, and my stage fright was very real. In fact, I actually became dizzy and faint, and one of the students had to get me some smelling salts! I had no idea how to control a class, or keep their interest or anything else. How Mr. Ryon ever decided I would be a suitable teacher I don't know. Furthermore, I was only twenty-three years old, and many of the students were as old as I was, some even older.[1]

Just staying ahead of the class required a great deal of study. He had an extremely heavy teaching schedule, typically nine lecture hours and 15 lab hours each week in three different subjects. He taught classes and supervised laboratory work for

Professor H.M. Morris at Rice Institute

a wide variety of engineering courses. At one time or another, he taught just about everything in the civil engineering curriculum. Professor Ryon supervised the content of these courses in general but for the most part left H.M. free to arrange the content, methods, grading, etc. It was very difficult, yet this varied experience proved invaluable in later years when H.M. became a department chairman.

In addition to his regular courses, he also taught night classes for the Engineering, Science, Management, and War Training program—surveying courses offered to civilians to help them develop useful skills for the war effort. Fortunately for his family, these courses provided H.M. a little extra income during difficult financial times.

Teaching required a great deal of time, but it was winning people to Christ that consumed H.M.'s heart. He was completely convinced God had brought him to Rice for that one purpose. When later asked for personal details to include on the cover of his first book, he told the publisher, "Really my interest and hobby, if it could be called such, is personal witnessing to the marvelous grace of the Lord Jesus Christ. I prefer, though, to consider that my occupation, with engineering as a sideline to pay expenses."[2] If his letters and appointment books tell the story, he urgently pursued this occupation.

From the moment they arrived at Rice, H.M. and Mary

Louise focused on introducing others to the Lord Jesus Christ. They joined South Main Baptist Church, where most Rice Baptist students attended. Soon they both taught Sunday school, served as officers of two adult classes, and participated in the Young Married Training Union. On campus, H.M. attended the daily meetings of the Baptist Student Union and

Professor H.M. Morris

soon became the faculty advisor. In addition to all this activity, they hosted a weekly Bible study at their home for students and friends from church.

The Gideons played an important role in H.M.'s spiritual growth. Their weekly and monthly meetings provided a rich source of fellowship for the couple. The Houston Gideons were especially active among servicemen downtown, and H.M. quickly became involved. Their work at the local Star of Hope downtown mission and the USO gave H.M. valuable training in evangelism methods and many opportunities to share his faith. Through these years at Rice, he led over 75 individuals to accept Christ as their Savior.

More importantly, H.M. began a practice of daily personal Bible study and prayer. He and his wife decided to daily read a devotional and pray together soon after their marriage, but here in Houston, with so many depending on his spiritual leadership, H.M. realized his own need for a deeper understanding of the Word and a closer relationship with the Lord. He began spending an hour early each morning in dedicated Bible study and earnest prayer, a practice he continued for the rest of his life.

H.M. also began a serious study of the creation/evolution questions. The years in El Paso rooted his faith in the truth of the Scriptures in a general way, but at Rice evolutionary dogma dominated all curricula. Surrounded by the almost universal disbelief in the scientific or historical accuracy of the Bible, H.M. realized that most students consequently graduated with indifferent, modernistic, or atheistic beliefs. Christian students were constantly challenged. Most compromised their faith because they accepted the arguments of theistic evolutionists and listened to the criticism of the Bible and Christianity.

God gave H.M. a bright and inquiring mind that insisted on finding answers to the big questions. His interest in the supposed conflict between science and the Bible began in El Paso when he first encountered Irwin Moon's teachings. He reasoned that scientific support for biblical creationism should be available and must be found if he was going to proclaim that the Bible was infallible.

H.M. searched the extensive scientific library at Rice, looking for every book available on the subject. Of that early investigation, he recalled:

> I read so many books during this period which advocated evolution—both atheistic and theistic books— that I almost reverted to belief in evolution myself. However, the advocated mechanism of mutation and natural selection never seemed adequate to explain it. Every time I would look at an insect or a tree or any living organism and then try to imagine how such a thing could ever be produced by mutation and nat-

ural selection, it seemed so absurdly impossible that the very idea almost made me angry! In fact it was these evolutionary books that eventually helped convince me that evolutionism was completely unscientific.[3]

His search took him to the local Baptist bookstore. Yet even there, "evolutionism seemed almost as prevalent in such officially-approved Southern Baptist literature as it did in the Rice library."[4]

Finally, he found the Bible, Tract, and Missionary Book Store, a biblical bookstore operated by a Plymouth Brethren businessman. H.M. quickly became its best patron, devouring any book on solid biblical exegesis—analyzing biblical texts— and especially anything related to science, history, or prophecy.

He found only a few books on scientific creationism by authors such as Harry Rimmer, Carl Schwarze, and Dr. Arthur I. Brown. They were encouraging but unconvincing. Searching for anything available on this topic, he ordered directly from publishers' lists and found books by Byron Nelson and Theodore Graebner, and—most significantly—George McCready Price, *The Modern Flood Theory of Geology*, which detailed the scientific implications of the great Flood.

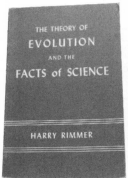 

Amazed at the wealth of valuable data and interpretations in this remarkable book, H.M. ordered all of Price's books and any other books by Adventist scientists that Price referred to. "Despite certain objectionable aspects to their theology, some of these Adventists—especially Price—provided an invaluable service to Biblical Christianity during the lean years of the 20's, 30's, and 40's."[5]

H.M. realized that one of the most difficult problems on this topic was the apparent age of the earth. All evolutionary books and most of the fundamentalist books seemed to accept that the earth was billions of years old. Some authors, like Rimmer, Schwarze, or Brown, advocated the gap theory, while others followed the day-age theory. Only a few Adventist writers seemed to favor a young earth, but even these were hesitant. Concerning this, H.M. wrote:

> For a while I tried to think through the Biblical and scientific implications of the various theories that Christians had proposed to harmonize the Bible with evolution and the geological ages. I seriously tried to accept theistic evolution and the day-age theory, and then later the gap theory. In fact, my first book offered the latter as at least a possible interpretation. However, the more I studied both science and Scripture, the more certain it became that such compromises were impossible. The Bible taught unequivocally that all things were made in six literal days only a few thousand years ago, and that was that![6]

During this time of intensive searching, he scoured the Bible verse by verse, listing every reference that had anything to do with creation and related subjects. Regardless of what most fundamentalists believed, he became more and more convinced that the Bible taught recent, literal creation, and it seemed completely impossible that the Bible could be the infallible Word of God if it was wrong on such a foundational issue. As a civil engineer with an increasing interest in hydraulics and hydrology, H.M. began to realize that geology and the Flood of the Bible were key to the scientific and historical validity of Scripture. It dawned on H.M. that the Lord might use his engineering and science interests. To this end, he sent letters to some of the Christian authors he had studied. He wrote to Carl Schwarze, a creationist engineering professor at New York University, to ask for guidance.

> I believe that God's will for my own life is leading along this line and am trying to make preparations for the future with that in view....God has given me a certain amount of engineering and scientific ability which I believe can and should be used in testifying to the truth of God's Word and the saving grace of the Lord Jesus Christ. Certainly there is no competition in this field, but rather a tremendous need for more men in every walk of life (especially science and engineering) to uplift Christ and the Bible to a God-forsaking, hell-bound world.[7]

He also discovered and joined the Creation-Deluge Society, beginning an ongoing correspondence with its president, Ben F. Allen, a highly motivated and vigorous proponent of Flood geology. This gentleman was very helpful throughout their correspondence, recognizing H.M.'s potential and encouraging his research.

During this time, H.M. was offered a position as Assistant Professor of Civil Engineering at Stanford University in California, with a raise of $400. Tempted, he almost gave in to the lure of the Golden State. However, he turned down the opportunity, still firmly convinced that God brought him to Rice for a specific purpose.

During this extended period of research, the most compelling force in H.M.'s life was the desire to reach the lost. His interest in science and creation provided many opportunities for speaking at various places, but one-on-one testimony and presentation of the gospel took precedence over everything else. He felt called to Rice for this reason, and he tried to fulfill his mission with remarkable energy and enthusiasm.

The home Bible class that he and Mary Louise hosted grew quite large. Since the Navy students occupied the dorms, he obtained permission from the Navy officer to hold the class on campus. They renamed it the Rice Christian Fellowship, and weekly meetings were held with various speakers. At one point, the famous apologist Dr. Harry Rimmer spoke to the class. At that time, he was considered the top defender of the scientific accuracy of the Bible and special creation. This earnest and enthusiastic evangelist created quite a stir wherever he spoke, and his message made a big impression on H.M.

God sent another influential Christian to Houston that year: Dawson Trotman of the Navigators, a ministry committed to reaching out to servicemen. He introduced the Navigator's Bible Memory Program as a more effective means of witnessing, and H.M. jumped in with both feet. Through the program, he memorized hundreds of Bible verses, which spurred his spiritual growth and became the ammunition for his personal witnessing. These verses were the backbone he relied on for every message he gave throughout his later career. Sometime later, the Gideons asked him to prepare their own memory program. With a few alterations, it is still in use today.

In addition, a representative of InterVarsity Christian Fellowship came to the campus. At the time, InterVarsity was

soundly orthodox as well as evangelistic, so the Rice Christian Fellowship voted to become a chapter, benefitting from InterVarsity leadership and methods. Many students made professions of faith, and the group became the most active religious organization on campus.

Testimony at the center

H.M. found many personal evangelism opportunities during his four years at Rice—weekly InterVarsity evangelistic meetings, ongoing efforts at the downtown mission, the United Service Organization, and individual contacts between professor and student. In addition, the Gideons organized the Houston Christian Servicemen's Center to have an impact on the thousands of servicemen passing through Houston. H.M. took a leadership role in all of these.

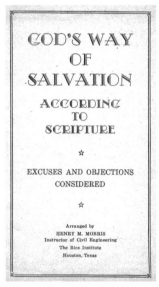

H.M.'s booklet (left); H.M. and mother Ida (right)

At the Servicemen's Center, H.M. coordinated evangelistic efforts. He arranged teams of workers each night, some standing outside inviting men to come in, others talking and counseling inside. Hostesses provided refreshments and recreation each evening. Even Ida began coming to the center to play the piano. All experienced tremendous blessing; over 1,000 soldiers made professions of faith during the last months of World War II.

Because of the need for a common message and method among the various Christian workers, H.M. put together a booklet containing salvation verses and a few answers to related questions. He titled it "God's Way of Salvation According to the Scripture" and had it printed by the thousands (see Appendix D). This tool was used at all these ministries and by local churches, and it also traveled overseas with servicemen. He wrote his brother Dick, who was stationed in the South Pacific:

> That reminds me; Mother said you read the little pamphlet I arranged. I sure hope you will use it, and try to learn the verses in it as well as you can. It is designed especially to help Christians know how to lead others to Christ. God has given me the privilege of winning quite a few servicemen and students to Christ in the past few months, and I can tell you that there is no thrill in this life that can compare with seeing some soul "pass from death unto life" through your testimony.[8]

This Christian publication by H.M. was the first of many. In fact, it was during these years of personal ministry and intense quest for the truth regarding science and the Bible that he sensed the need for a book geared toward college students. Through his experience in witnessing, he recognized the stumbling block that science placed in the path of a young person considering salvation. Reflecting on this time, he later commented:

> As I learned more and more in the Scriptures, and also more and more concerning the supposed scientific and other fallacies in the Scriptures, I became impressed with the need for a new forthright book on Christian evidences, especially one written by an

evangelical scientist. With only a B.S. degree, I really didn't qualify as a recognized scientist, but there were apparently no others at that time. Harry Rimmer was mainly a theologian, George McCready Price was a self-taught geologist and a Seventh-Day Adventist, Arthur I. Brown was a former medical doctor turned Bible conference speaker, Rendle Short was a British surgeon who compromised on geology and supported the day-age theory, Theodore Schwarze a retired civil engineering professor. Books by these men were about all I had been able to find in those days, and none of them were really satisfactory. Consequently, I was presumptuous enough to think that maybe I could begin writing a book. In a way, I was a frustrated journalist anyhow and liked to write.[9]

He began to work in earnest on this idea, pulling together evidences and arguments from many places and sources. Sometime in the summer of 1944, he finished a manuscript called *That You Might Believe* and looked to several trusted mentors to review it—pastor Dr. Yearby of his church in El Paso, Stacey Woods of InterVarsity Christian Fellowship, pastor Dick Seume of his church in Houston, and Gideon friend Dr. W.S. Mosher. All agreed it could have an impact on students.

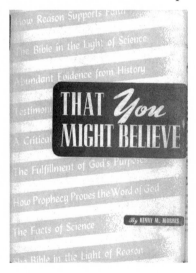

Stacey Woods sent it to a tract-printing business called Good News Publishing. Since this company was just about to enter the book publishing arena, they accepted it. *That You Might Believe* became the first book the organization printed.

However, the contract required that H.M. purchase the first 500 copies. With no extra money, this seemed like an overwhelming obstacle. The Lord overcame this problem through a well-to-do Gideon friend. Mr. W.S. Mosher of the Mosher Steel Company underwrote the book and even decided that the 500 copies should be given away to students and others who would promise to read it.

The book was published in the spring of 1946, and H.M. had the joy of giving complimentary copies to all the InterVarsity students, all the students in his classes, the Rice faculty, and anyone who requested a copy with the promise to read it. It was extremely well-received and seemed to make an impact at Rice in the final months of H.M.'s four years on the faculty. He wrote his publisher about the many positive responses and especially of the conversion of a couple of agnostics.

> As far as I have heard thus far, there has been no one that has been critical or unconvinced by the contents. Although the book is not at all an advanced, scholarly work, and will thus probably not appeal to mature apologists, I hope and believe it will fill a real need, previously unfilled, for a book to give unsaved or uncertain college and high school students who are plagued with intellectual difficulties, and to bring them out of the morass of doubt onto the rock of Christian assurance.[10]

That You Might Believe bore wonderful fruit, but H.M.'s enthusiasm over its reception was naïve and short-lived. It was not long before his books became fodder for much scorn and persecution from evolutionists, agnostics, and even other Christians. The book was the first small step onto a new battlefield—one that took great effort, demanded much personal sacrifice, and engendered a complete dependence on the One who called him.

As H.M. continued to grow professionally and spiritually, his family grew as well. Kathleen "Kathy" Louise was born on August 10, 1944, at almost the same time his brother John Robert was killed in the war. They committed her to the Lord, with the sure conviction that the Bible was the very Word of God and provided all necessary instruction for shaping the lives of their children.

Henry III, Kathleen, and Mary Louise

The couple's spiritual growth was evident in many ways. Through various circumstances during these years at Rice, and through the application of biblical principles for guidance, they gradually became convinced that many of their social practices were inconsistent with an effective Christian testimony. Their desire for spiritual depth led them to join a different church, Berachah Church, which had excellent teaching and edifying fellowship. H.M.'s mother Ida soon joined, became a regular pianist, and began to grow in the Lord also. When his brother Dick returned from the war, he and his wife Helen attended as well.

Those who knew H.M. considered him to be humble, gracious, and approachable. Yet he learned a valuable lesson in his zeal for the faith. When Dick first became engaged to Helen, they were new believers in Christ. After spending time with H.M. and Mary Louise, Helen had reservations about her newfound faith and fitting in this family. She wrote Dick, then stationed in the South Pacif-

Richard "Dick" Morris

ic, that she was breaking their engagement. She felt she could never be considered one of the family because she was not as passionate about "religion" as the rest. Desperate, Dick wrote H.M., asking him to please intervene and let Helen know he and the rest of the family would not judge her. H.M. sent a letter of apology to Helen. She accepted, and the engagement resumed. He learned that one's speech must "be always with grace, seasoned with salt" (Colossians 4:6). By wielding his sword with such abandon, he had wounded his dear brother. Gentle persuasion, not passionate pursuit, became H.M.'s most effective weapon.

9

Sharpening the Edge

By 1946, the war was over, and Rice was phasing out its Navy program. H.M. knew God was calling him to be a teacher. His passion was to preach "nothing save the cross," but more and more he realized God was preparing and equipping him to bear testimony to the educational and scientific communities. His mental strengths, if honed and sharpened by the Spirit, would enable him to give an *apologia*—a systematic defense and reason of the hope within him (1 Peter 3:15).

This "sharpening" involved more education. He needed an advanced degree. Professor Ryon, his supervisor, advised him there was no opportunity for advancement at Rice. With a wife, two children, and a baby on the way, H.M. needed to find a job somewhere near a suitable graduate school so he could pursue his degree part-time. This was a daunting prospect to a husband and father just 28 years old.

The previous few years of Bible study, prayer, and personal evangelism taught H.M. to lean on the Lord for direction and provision, so it was with confidence he turned his face toward a new goal. He determined that the best field to pursue was hydraulics. With his experience at the Boundary Commission in El Paso and a personal preference for that branch of civil engineering, it seemed the logical choice. More importantly, it would serve as the best background for studying the evidences of the Genesis Flood, which he "now was firmly convinced constituted the most critical area in the relation between science and the Bible."[1]

The University of Minnesota and the University of Iowa hosted outstanding hydraulics graduate programs. However, his best prospect of employment seemed to be at the Illinois Institute of Technology in Chicago, where his old supervisor from the Boundary Commission directed fluid mechanics research. H.M. inquired and was invited up for an interview in July 1946. The International Gideon Convention was also meeting that summer in Minneapolis, so he arranged a train trip to investigate the three schools and enjoy the convention's spiritual blessings.

Henry III, Mary Louise, and Kathy

At the convention, H.M. benefitted greatly from the fellowship and friendship of godly mentors. In addition, the University of Minnesota immediately offered H.M. a full-time instructorship and admission to their graduate program.

Confident that it was the Lord's choice, H.M. accepted the position. He planned to work on a master's degree in hydraulics. He hoped to minor in geology, but his degree required a minor in mathematics. Eventually, his supervisor, a specialist in sedimentation mechanics research, agreed that the geology profession badly needed the insights of fluid mechanics and hydrology and approved an interdisciplinary approach. However, H.M. had only read a number of geology books; he had never taken a geology class. After he reassured the administration that he would, by outside reading, learn the subject matter for the prerequisites (e.g., mineralogy) to the graduate courses he wanted to take (geomorphology, sedimentation, etc.), they allowed him to continue. The Lord was evidently leading in all of this—years later, H.M. acknowledged that this was the best combination of courses he could have taken for future contributions in scientific creationism.[2]

So, the Morris family crammed their belongings into Belinda—the nickname now applied to a '41 Chevy coupe— and headed for the land of snowdrifts and frozen lakes. This presented quite a change from the land of high humidity and heat. They soon became acquainted with snow shovels, sleds, ice scrapers, and mittens.

H.M. and Belinda II

They arrived in St. Paul when the city was experiencing a population boom and a serious housing shortage. However, the Lord provided a faculty apartment in Thatcher Hall where they lived the first year.

Shortly after they arrived, an incident occurred that had great significance for H.M.'s future ministry. Dr. Arthur I. Brown was holding a Bible conference, and as he was one of only a handful of men at that time who had written anything on scientific creationism, H.M. immediately went to meet him. He discovered that Dr. Brown had not only read his book *That You Might Believe* but was recommending it at his meetings. H.M. made an appointment with Dr. Brown to ask for advice concerning his future.

With the rising threat of communism in those days after World War II, many Christians felt the return of Christ must be very near. H.M. seriously questioned whether it was wise to spend so many years on graduate studies when it would be more eternally valuable to dedicate his time to evangelism before it was too late. He was hoping Dr. Brown would advise him not to waste his time on education but to get busy winning souls—which is what he preferred anyway.

However, Dr. Brown advised him to get his Ph.D. He assured H.M. that his ministry would be far more effective in the long run and that there was a great need for solid testimony in the scientific and educational worlds. With the proper credentials, H.M. just might well be one whom God would use to meet that need.

H.M. freely repeated those words to his own children and all that asked him the same question over the next 60 years. He frequently used the phrase "occupy till I come," referring to Christ's parable to His disciples when they "thought that the kingdom of God should immediately appear" (Luke 19:11-13).

At the office in Minnesota

Other surprises and blessings were in store for the Morris family. As they visited parks, restaurants, and other public places, they were mystified that they saw few other children in the city. On their first trip to a large church in downtown Minneapolis, they learned that there was no nursery. They realized, to their dismay, that Minneapolis was in the throes of a serious polio epidemic, and no one was taking children out in public! There was nothing for them to do but pray.

On the positive side, Minneapolis had a thriving Christian community. Many excellent churches and several Bible colleges were established there, and a number of faithful Christian faculty members worked at the university.

H.M. quickly became involved in Minneapolis' InterVarsity chapter. It was the largest in the nation but not as passionately evangelistic as the one at Rice. Although he attended the weekly InterVarsity meetings faithfully, he and several of the engineering students started a subdivision of the chapter called the Engineers' Christian Fellowship, where they were able to reach a good number of students in that department for Christ.

The family soon joined the Powderhorn Park Baptist Church, and H.M. began teaching the college class there. The group grew

quite large because of the various Bible colleges in the area. The excellent preaching of Pastor Wallace Olson and the fellowship of many strong Christians at the church made the family's five and a half years in Minnesota especially enjoyable and edifying.

They met another Christian couple who also just joined the faculty and lived in Thatcher Hall. Together they began a Bible study class for faculty in the apartment building. Several of the faculty men and their wives became Christians through that ministry. H.M. was surprised to find that a significant number of Bible-believing Christians served on the faculty. This was very different from what he had experienced at Rice. He had come to believe that Christian professors hardly existed and that evolutionary intellectualism and humanism had completely taken over the world of secular higher education. Although none of the faculty were strong creationists, it was at least encouraging that quite a few of them believed the Bible was God's Word.

Graduate students came from all over the world to study hydraulics or other branches of civil engineering at this university, and H.M. spent much of his free time in ministry to them. His position provided ideal opportunities for foreign missionary work right from his own office. Lonely and interested in American culture, these students gladly accepted his invitation to go with him to church. Often, H.M. dropped the family off at church and then returned to pick up as many as he could fit in his Chevy. (The record was 11.)

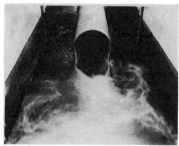

St. Anthony Falls Hydraulics Laboratory

In addition to these ministries, family life, and graduate studies, H.M. was assigned to instruct several survey courses. Later, he taught fluid mechanics, hydrology, applied hydraulics, structural analysis, and other subjects. These were busy times for him!

The University of Minnesota hosted the St. Anthony Falls Hydraulics Laboratory, a facility built on the Mississippi River and powered by the 50-foot falls. H.M. received an appointment at the lab first to do extensive research on the hydraulics of culverts sponsored by the U.S. Bureau of Public Roads, then later to study pipe and culvert hydraulics sponsored by the American Concrete Pipe Association. He later wrote:

> As project leader on these studies, I was able to get a number of good publications out, which gave me something of a reputation as an authority on the subject of flow in pipes and channels. These publications stressed more the practical design and commercial applications for the sponsor's benefit, but the measurements and analyses also enabled me to develop the ideas for a completely new approach to the hydraulic analysis of flow over rough surfaces, such as the corrugated metal culvert pipes we were studying.[3]

This analysis became the basis for his dissertation topic— "A New Concept of Flow in Rough Conduits."

> As far as the theoretical development was concerned, it proceeded well, but very definitely with the Lord's help. I prayed often about it, and the Lord answered. Over and over again, I had the thrilling experience of coming to a seeming impasse, then praying about it, and then suddenly seeing how to solve the problem.[4]

The dissertation became the basis for journal articles published in the scientific literature and was eventually widely known around the world. Much later, he incorporated the theory into his textbook on applied hydraulics, and it became part of the standard basic knowledge of subsequent hydraulic engineers.

> I doubt if anyone ever had an easier time in producing a doctoral dissertation in this field, and there have been few that have become more widely known or influential. There were so many providential aspects to it, however, that I realize very little credit belongs to me for it. It was God's blessing and guidance, and apparently He wanted to hurry me on to more important matters. The dissertation, the experience, the publications—even the degree itself—were merely the necessary preparation and credentials for a future ministry of more eternal significance.[5]

The evidence of God's involvement filled H.M. with confidence to continue toward his goal. He knew that all those who would serve the King with effectiveness must go through training. He recognized that the Holy Spirit was his chief teacher. There were also many more mature believers who took an interest in him and gave him wise counsel.

During H.M.'s time at Rice, he began contacting various scientists and apologists, gaining insight along the way. One of these learned individuals was Ben F. Allen, who led the Creation-Deluge Society, an organization dedicated to researching the relationship between the global Flood of Noah's day and creation as taught in the Bible. Allen's correspondence with H.M. was very helpful and encouraging. He wrote:

God has greatly blessed you with an exceptional balance between true personal evangelism and true science. (And I am coming to recognize such a combination of gifts as rare indeed), God-given for our day....No greater call of God seems possible in this our day, or more crucial, for leading "leading" people to God, for today many leading people are confused by "science falsely so-called." Effective evangelism of today demands just this duplex gift....

Your work there (in Minnesota), both major and minor, fits right into a job that I have known for years should be done, and on which I have notes and conceptions. Of all the things that WATER did during the Deluge, it clearly was TORRENTIAL in many places in all parts of the earth....Features cannot be found "in process" today, and must be studied as deposits of the Deluge, if they are to be fully understood. But they must be fully understood by the civil engineer who is dealing with Deluge strata in excavations of all sorts.[6]

Letters like this firmly cemented H.M.'s interest in hydraulics as a key to understanding geology and its significance in the debate concerning the age of the earth. Another Christian apologist, Molleurus Couperus, stoked the "fire in his belly" by writing:

As I see it, the men who are capable of carrying the true light of the relation of science and revelation to the world are required by God to do so, their particular burden. Never before has our opportunity been better than today, and may God help us to discharge our responsibility.[7]

H.M.'s book *That You Might Believe* was published in the spring of 1946 and received many wonderful reviews. Quite a few readers sent letters telling how they came to believe in Christ after reading it. By 1948, the book was well into its second printing, and a third was planned. This success encouraged H.M. to continue writing, and he wrote a booklet titled *The Biblical Evidence for a Recent Creation and Worldwide Deluge.* He sent the manuscript to several trusted apologists and received some unexpected advice.

Dr. Wilbur Smith, a famous Bible scholar from Moody Bible Institute, analyzed and critiqued virtually every paragraph and wrote:

> Parts of it are incontrovertible; other parts seem to be theory suspended in the air. We have not fully wrestled with all this problem; we need a man who knows chemistry, physics, geology, paleontology, and the Bible, to get into the subject with thoroughness and give us a great book on it. Why don't you do it? You have a way of carefully investigating subjects, but it should be gone into with a vast amount of research.[8]

Smith recommended that the book not be published yet, and he was not alone in his analysis. Dr. Arthur I. Brown wrote:

> I hope my comments on your article were not too drastic....But, I was anxious that you should study a bit further before you placed your ideas before the public, feeling in my own mind, that, afterwards you would regret it.[9]

Dr. J. Oliver Buswell from The National Bible Institute in New York read his book and wrote a scathing and sarcastic critique about the lack of footnotes and references to previous apologetic works.[10]

However, H.M.'s stated intention was to write short, easily finished books for the curious or doubting college student. With his intense schedule of graduate studies and teaching, a more complete project had to be put off. Besides, a new opportunity captured his interest.

During his involvement with foreign students and frequent missionary speakers at church, H.M. and Mary Louise seriously considered the possibility of foreign missions. His passion for evangelism was intense, and the idea of serving as a "nonprofessional missionary" in a teaching capacity at a foreign university was compelling.

Reason *and the Christian Hope*

Can we know that Christianity is true?

Just as these thoughts were taking hold, a seemingly providential door opened. Dick Soderberg, a high school science teacher who taught in an experimental, United Nations-sponsored school in Kabul, Afghanistan, convinced the Afghan government to establish an engineering college in Kabul. Soderberg was a committed Christian and determined to secure Christian teachers for the faculty. The country was completely closed to missionaries—Afghanistan's Islamic laws forbade Christians to preach. Mr. Soderberg hoped to bring Christians in as faculty and establish a beachhead there with the gospel. He traveled to America and, hearing of a young mission-minded engineer, came to Minneapolis to recruit H.M.

H.M. and Mary Louise, Kathy, John, and Henry III

Taking a family of small children into an undeveloped and hostile land was a daunting prospect, but both H.M. and Mary Louise felt the Lord had opened this door. In January 1949, they agreed to go. They planned to leave in the fall of 1950, which required H.M. to complete his Ph.D. on an accelerated timetable.

Two years later, by March 1951, the door closed. The Afghanistan government decided to postpone the engineering college and set up a vocational institute instead. Disappointed, yet somewhat relieved, H.M. and Mary Louise realized God used this to bring them to a complete dedication to His will, no matter the cost. H.M. remembered in retrospect:

> Although we were willing to go, Mary Louise and I really couldn't help being thankful that the Lord finally led in other ways. Knowing our own limitations, it seemed clear that we were hardly qualified to

serve as missionaries in such an isolated and primitive culture as Afghanistan. For one thing, though, the experience of praying and preparing for it proved a blessing to our children, especially to Kathleen, who would eventually become a missionary in an even more primitive land.[11]

By this time, the family had grown to four children. H.M. and Mary Louise quickly learned that they must depend on the Lord for all physical, spiritual, and financial needs.

H.M.'s salary at the university barely covered their minimum needs, and at the birth of their third child, John David, it was impossible to save for hospital bills. John was born on December 7, 1946, and at the same time the two older kids, Henry III and Kathy, both contracted chicken pox. That meant Mary Louise could leave the hospital but John must stay for several more days to avoid exposure. With a much larger bill than expected, they needed to take out a loan. They prayed fervently, and on the very day that John was to be discharged, an unexpected check arrived in the mail. It was the very first royalty check for H.M.'s first book, *That You Might Believe*, and it was exactly $1 more than the hospital bill!

H.M. with mother Ida, Kathy, and John

Ida and son

In October 1948, another answer to prayer came in the form of a seeming miracle. Ida came for a visit, and while in Minnesota she had a series of heart attacks. The last one was very severe, and it appeared to be fatal. The hospital called H.M. to come immediately, but on the way he was delayed about 15 minutes by a long freight train. He prayed urgently for his mother while he waited.

When he finally arrived at the hospital, the doctors and nurses rushed to him and exclaimed that they had seen a miracle! Ida's heart stopped beating for several minutes, and they thought she was dead. However, her heart suddenly began beating again. When she regained consciousness, she told a remarkable story. She remembered being aware of leaving her body and thought she was about to be transported to heaven. She could see it in the distance and was enraptured by the beautiful lights and music. She was even aware of her son Bobby, killed four years previously in the war, waiting for her. Then she recalled going back to the hospital and seeing the doctors and nurses working over her body.

This story was repeated often in the family, accompanied by praises and wonder, and sometimes skepticism. No one really understood what it meant, and H.M. said:

I really don't know how to evaluate this dream or whatever the experience may have been, especially in the light of similar stories told in recent years even by non-Christians, as heart massage techniques have been developed to produce similar recoveries. The doctor considered it a miracle and Mother continued to live for 35 years afterwards. Although she had several strokes and other physical infirmities, they did not incapacitate her, and she never had another heart attack. In fact, on one occasion, when she had a bad gallbladder attack, the doctor thought it might be her heart. However, on thorough examination, he said that her heart indeed seemed to be in excellent condition, with no evidence whatever that she had ever had a heart attack at all![12]

Andrew "Andy" Hunter Morris born in 1949 (left);
Mary Ruth added to the family in 1951 (right)

Mary Louise gave birth to Andrew Hunter Morris in 1949 and Mary Ruth on Valentine's Day 1951. Both Henry III and Kathy were baptized at Powderhorn Baptist Church and continued to grow in spiritual understanding. While H.M. maintained a complex schedule, his wife maintained their busy household. Even with five children, Mary Louise taught a Good News Bible Club for the neighborhood children, furthering the spiritual growth of her children and their friends.

Morris children playing in the snow (left); H.M. and Andy (right)

In December 1950, H.M. became Dr. Henry M. Morris. He was 32 years old, and his career was just beginning. Convinced the Lord was leading him, he intended to promote creationism and the biblical perspective in the academic world. He sensed that God had enabled him to complete the particular courses and obtain the graduate degrees to help establish true faith in the biblical record of creation.

Dr. H.M. Morris

The Christian world at that time seemed more inclined than ever to capitulate to evolution, with the inevitable yielding of biblical inerrancy. Creationists were ridiculed by Christian intellectuals, and the surrender of fundamentalism to the rising neo-evangelical movement seemed certain.[13] H.M. did not know what, if anything, could be done about these disheartening trends, but he knew that the Lord was still sovereign and His Word was true. He believed God would do something, and he wanted to be that well-tempered and sharpened sword should God choose to use him.

Henry III in Minneapolis

10

The Sparks Fly

While still a young professional, H.M. gained recognition as an energetic professor and scholarly researcher. Several universities took notice, but Louisiana State University seemed the most promising. It was a well-known university and a good place for H.M. to have a meaningful testimony as a creationist. However, another school, the Southwestern Louisiana Institute, also inquired about his availability. After visiting both, H.M. was offered a position at Louisiana State as Assistant Professor, but to his amazement Southwestern offered him the position of Civil Engineering Department Head with the title of full Professor. The engineering program was unaccredited and needed a Ph.D. with broad teaching experience in civil engineering to redesign the entire curriculum to bring it up to accreditable caliber.

After much prayer and counsel, H.M. determined that this position at Southwestern Louisiana Institute, though extremely challenging for one inexperienced in administration, was what God wanted him to take. Once again leaving many Christian friends and a wonderful church, the family headed south in their 1941 Chevy coupe, even more crowded this time, in June 1951.

Southwestern Louisiana Institute (now the University of Louisiana at Lafayette) was in what was known as "Evangeline country," named after the heroine of Henry Wadsworth Longfellow's epic poem describing the 18th-century journey of French Acadians from Nova Scotia to Louisiana's bayou region. Their descendants, the Cajuns, dominated the region with their distinctive culture and musical dialect.

H.M. as head of Civil Engineering Dept. at Southwestern Louisiana Institute

Lafayette had a population of only about 35,000 and because of the French heritage was probably about 90% Catholic. This move proved to be a drastic change for a family coming from a prestigious university and one of the best-known evangelical communities in the country.

After settling the family into an apartment near the campus, H.M. went to work reorganizing the engineering department. To his dismay, it had undergone bitter rivalry among the faculty members, and several resigned because of H.M.'s appointment. Not only the curriculum but the faculty as well had to be almost completely reorganized.

The lab facilities were minimal and the budget quite low, but through creative additions the department was able to sufficiently cover the basic engineering mechanics. Over the next few years, they added faculty and many new courses. It took two attempts, but by 1955 it was a very respectable undergraduate program and accreditation was achieved. This success and the experience he acquired in administration later helped H.M. to gain a better position in a much larger university.

Soon after arriving in Lafayette, the family joined the First Baptist Church, one of the few Protestant churches in the area. The pastor was godly and well-meaning, but the church was not as dedicated to fundamental principles as their previous churches. H.M. once again taught an adult Sunday school class and later assumed the role of deacon in the church and faculty advisor to the Baptist Student Union on campus. Both H.M. and Mary Louise believed God brought them to this very needy community, and they seized many opportunities to witness for Christ on campus, in various church activities, and in their neighborhood. However, their most important and effective work seemed to be through the Gideons.

The Gideons organization was one of the instruments God used in H.M.'s life in El Paso and at Rice to bring about spiritual growth, fostering a love and respect for the Bible and its absolute necessity for effective ministry. He had not been very active in the Gideons while in Minneapolis—that city was given much "light" and the Bible was commonly available.

However, Lafayette was different. It was the hub city of what was called the "citadel of Catholicism" in the United States. H.M. wrote to a friend, "There is certainly no place in this country, and probably not many in the

Morris home in Lafayette

world, in greater darkness than is south Louisiana."[1] The Bible was almost unknown. Most had never read it, and many had never even seen a copy. Because the Word of God is essential to salvation, it seemed to H.M. that the first priority was to sow the seed of the Word as widely as possible. He determined to start a Gideon camp—local chapter—in Lafayette.

H.M. wrote to the Gideons southern zone leaders for advice and then contacted Christian businessmen in Lafayette. Gradually, he persuaded several about the Bible's importance, and a few met for Sunday morning breakfast, prayer, and devotions. The men began to grow spiritually, and they gained permission to place Bibles in hotels and hospitals. They held the first-ever street meeting in the town, held Bible dedication services, and participated in radio interviews. By 1952, there were 16 Gideons in the group, and all sensed God was beginning something big in this dark corner of the world.

However, they encountered opposition at every attempt to make the Word of God available to the community. The Roman Catholic clergy strongly resisted their efforts. When Bibles were distributed among the college ROTC unit, the clergy ordered faithful Catholics to get rid of them. Through their influence, the schools were completely closed to the Scriptures. H.M. later recalled:

> The Catholic hierarchy controlled all the school boards and did not want their young people confused by the Bible, especially the Protestant Bible! Finally, however, we were able to get permission to place Testaments in Crowley's high school one year. Crowley was the least Catholic of the cities of our area (only about 60%—near the western edge of Louisiana's Cajun country). We had to leave the Testaments in

the principal's offices, where the students could come get them if they wished. As it turned out, the offices were practically mobbed with young people trying to get copies of God's Word! The next day, however, there was a great Bible-burning in Crowley, as the priests forced many students to give them up to the bonfires.[2]

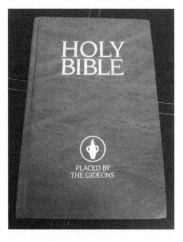

On another occasion, Gideon testaments were offered through a Protestant teacher in St. Martinsville, possibly the most Catholic town in the area. Although most of the students went to Catholic catechism classes, this teacher had just a few Protestant students in her religion class. For this reason, she was allowed a supply of testaments for her students. When the Catholic students heard of this from their friends, large numbers of them went to her home to get testaments for themselves. This led to many fierce reactions and even threats from the Catholic clergy.

The efforts of the Catholic priests intensified, and they sought fervently to prevent the distribution of the Bible. It seemed like an Old World atmosphere in which the priests attempted to control the minds of the people. They used insults, slander, and even death threats to prevent H.M. and the Gideons from spreading the Protestant gospel.

It almost came to violence on one occasion. A young Baptist preacher pastoring a small church in a French Catholic community planned to meet with a church member and his Catholic friend to discuss the Bible. The friend invited his priest to the discussion. The young Baptist preacher, feeling inadequate to deal with a priest, asked H.M. to come. H.M. reported later to his mother:

> In the meantime, the ones in the community began to publicize the thing, the priest announced it from his pulpit, etc., and the whole community began to be stirred up about it. The Catholics arranged for some priests to come up from the Seminary in Lafayette. They sent for newspaper reporters, and told them to come and see the Baptists get their mouths shut once and for all. When Cleve (the young preacher) found things had taken this turn…he asked three French Baptist missionaries who are in the general area to come too. They had been involved in similar affairs in the past, and they said that, without exception, the Catholics would never permit the discussion to be fair, but would interfere in every way they could and, in the old days, would often resort to physical violence, bringing guns, knives, and everything to the meetings. They all felt that it could not accomplish any good, but at the same time felt we could not back down from it.
>
> …I had not made much preparation, as I had thought it was just going to be a private discussion with a few people present. You can imagine how I felt when I found the true situation. We went on over to the place, and found about fifty Baptists and about 150 Catholics waiting. There were four priests there. The Catholics were at the house of the man that had started the thing; the Baptists were at a house nearby….

One of the French Baptist preachers had invited the sheriff to come to keep order and to see that the discussion was carried on according to reasonable rules. Just about time for us to go over to the house where the Catholics were, one of our men went over to ask if they were ready for us to come. The priests told him they had decided against having the meeting at all. The sheriff came up about then and we asked him to go over there to find out if that was really the case, as a witness, to guard against their spreading the story that the Baptists had backed out. He went, and after quite a bit of time, came back and said that yes, the priests did not want to hold the discussion. It was prayer meeting night, so we just had a service out in the open. One of the French preachers had brought loudspeakers along, so he set them up and preached a Gospel sermon, in French, which must have been heard by the whole countryside.

I don't know, of course, but I rather think that the sheriff's presence was what made the Catholics decide not to have the meeting.[3]

Finally, a breakthrough occurred. One of the Gideons who was on good terms with the local bishop offered to buy a supply of the Roman Catholic Confraternity Testaments if the Gideons were allowed to go to the schools and offer students a choice between that and the Gideon Testament. Surprisingly, the bishop gave his consent, and immediately doors that once seemed impossible to enter opened to the Word. Although it was primarily a sowing rather than a reaping ministry, the seeds sowed led to a gradual opening of the whole area after being so long destitute of the Word of God.

Many other opportunities for evangelism and teaching cropped up. As Southwestern Louisiana Institute faculty advisor for the Baptist Student Union, H.M. increased activities on campus. The group had become ineffectual in evangelism because of the opposition of the Catholic faculty, so H.M. organized an InterVarsity chapter on the campus to help spread the gospel.

However, the Catholic administrators erected barriers against InterVarsity that were almost insurmountable. Even the Protestant churches opposed it, thinking it would diminish the denominational organizations on campus. Members from his own Baptist church were particularly hurtful in their slander, fearing competition for the Baptist Student Union. Eventually the Southwestern Louisiana Institute administration authorized the organization, and a small group of faithful students began to witness on campus, although they were only authorized to recruit from students who had indicated no church preference on their "religious preference" cards.

The InterVarsity group struggled through the next few years, finally seeing some growth among foreign students. The greatest weakness in this effort as well as other campus interdenominational Christian organizations was the lack of affiliation with a good church. H.M. noted, "The problem, however, is too often the fact (as in this case) that there is no nearby church with both the doctrinal soundness and evangelistic burden for students that the situation requires."[4]

In spite of all the opposition from friends and foes alike, they reached many students with the gospel, and distributed many Bibles. H.M. was also able to give copies of the new edition of *That You Might Believe*, retitled *The Bible and Modern Science*, to help build a strong foundation for their faith in God's Word.

Many off-campus opportunities for evangelism arose, as well as for in-depth Bible teaching. H.M. frequently spoke at the Baptist church services and special study courses. He was elected state president of the Gideons and traveled often to speak at conventions, rallies, and dedications. He also visited prisons and flood relief camps for evangelistic meetings. Through the Gideons, and because of his book, H.M. gradually became known throughout the state and was often asked to speak, almost always on the subject of science and the Bible.

At one event at the state penitentiary, there were 250 professions of faith. His son Henry III, now 12, accompanied him to this presentation to play the accordion. While H.M. and others were trying to meet and counsel those who came forward, Henry III disappeared. They found him in the prison yard questioning prisoners about their faith. His father's zeal for evangelism had taken root in his own young heart.

In spite of all the fruit from personal evangelism and teaching, H.M. suspected that the most important contribution he could make to the Lord's work was to address the crumbling foundation of the modern church and its views on science and the Bible. He needed to continue his research and writing on the manuscript that he had begun while in Minneapolis. He hoped it would eventually become a thoroughly documented and definitive scientific exposition of creation and the Flood. But the immediate needs around him demanded his time, and he made little progress on the manuscript. He wrote a friend:

> Well, I hope some day to find time to finish my book, started about six or so years ago, and which I optimistically conceive as a *magnum opus*, giving a complete Biblical and geological exposition based on the literal interpretation of the Genesis records of creation and the Flood. I intend this year to devote special efforts to finding time for this work, setting aside other things as far as possible. I trust that such would be honoring to the Lord and His Word, and that He will grant the needed grace and ability for such a work.[5]

H.M.'s involvement with the American Scientific Affiliation, a Christian organization committed to creationism and the Bible, gave the extra push he needed to delve deeper into his research. He first learned of the organization and joined in 1948, hoping to stay in contact with other scientists who believed in Scripture's accuracy and authority. However, he soon discovered the compromising position American Scientific Affiliation held on evolution and the Bible. Most of its members had capitulated to Darwinism and accepted either the gap theory (ruin and reconstruction) or the day-age theory (each creation day represented a separate age). H.M. became the self-described "chief gadfly" of the American Scientific Affiliation, agitating unsuccessfully to get leadership to seriously consider Flood geology. He felt if they could only see that the Scriptures taught a recent creation in six literal days, followed by the worldwide effects of the Curse and then the cataclysmic, world-destroying Deluge, they would modify their scientific interpretations accordingly.[6] He knew their compromising views on evolution would ultimately diminish their view of God. He wrote to one American Scientific Affiliation member, Dr. Edward Carnell of Fuller Theological Seminary, who agreed with him and had recently written an article titled "Beware of the New Deism."

> I suppose I am one of the few in the A.S.A. who believes in these things. However, it appears quite impossible to me to believe in anything other than a recent creation and universal deluge if one is also going to believe in plenary verbal inspiration of Scripture. Of course, the principle of uniformity must be rejected if there really was a creation of all things in six literal days and a subsequent aqueous destruction of the world that then was. The modern uniformitarians, and their rejection of a real creation and Deluge, are succinctly described in II Peter 3:3-6.[7]

At the American Scientific Affiliation 1953 convention held at Grace College and Seminary in Winona Lake, Indiana, H.M. presented a paper titled "Biblical Evidence for a Recent Creation and Universal Deluge." Although a few agreed with his position, the great majority rejected it without even attempting to refute the overwhelming biblical evidence for a literal recent creation and a universal flood. Acceptance of the geologic-age system was more important than believing the Bible.

The paper was also printed in the InterVarsity magazine *His*. Both printings produced strong negative reactions from Christian intellectuals. He wrote Stacey Woods, his friend and president of InterVarsity Christian Fellowship, concerning the importance of this problem:

> This may seem to many, possibly even to you, like a rather trivial question. Perhaps it is, but it seems to me to reflect a very important question of men-

tal and spiritual attitude. Not only that, but it seems to me that the philosophy of evolutionary development is at the very center of all anti-Christian and anti-Biblical systems. The theory of evolution draws its only real evidence from historical geology and, in the minds of most people at least, once the orthodox framework of geologic ages is granted, evolution necessarily follows as an implication. Consequently, the reality or non-reality of these geologic ages is a very important problem. In the last century, Christendom quickly accepted the geologic ages as taught by Cuvier and Lyell, adopting the day-age theory, for the most part, as a supposed means of harmonizing Genesis with geology. This situation made it very easy, then, for the transition into theistic evolution and finally into outright modernism on the part of most of the churches of the immediate past generation. I am afraid that this history will be repeated on the part of present evangelical churches if our present tendency of continual retreat under scientific theories goes on.[8]

The criticism from the members of American Scientific Affiliation and other Christian philosophers cemented in H.M.'s mind the need for a thoroughly documented book on the effects of the universal Flood and its relevance to science and the Bible.

Though H.M.'s paper faced much opposition at the 1953 convention, a young theologian from Grace Seminary, John Whitcomb, heard it and wrote to request copies for his class.

I greatly appreciated your paper on a Recent Creation and Universal Deluge which you read at the A.S.A. convention. I feel that your conclusions are scripturally valid, and therefore must be sustained by a fair examination of geologic evidence in time to come. My only regret is that so few trained Christian men of science are willing to let God's Word have the final say on these questions....I have adopted your views, as well as those of Rehwinkle, Nelson, and Price, and am presenting them to my class as preferable alternatives to the gap-theory and the day-age theory.

Sincerely in Christ,

John C. Whitcomb, Jr, Associate Prof. of O.T., Grace Theological Seminary[9]

H.M. replied:

It is very encouraging to have found that there are a number of other very capable Christian scholars who believe that the Scriptural evidence requires acceptance of a literal, six-day creation and a subsequent universal Deluge, regardless of ephemeral geological theories.

I have been trying to write a book of my own for some time....I hope to find time to get this work finished this year, but there are so many other things continually pressing on one's time. I would surely appreciate your prayers about this.[10]

Correspondence continued between the two, with exchanges from Whitcomb on Hebrew exposition and his plans for his doctoral dissertation.

I appreciate your fine letter, and trust that I may be of further help in any way. I am planning to write my doctor's dissertation on the subject of your paper, so would appreciate any further references you might have at hand.[11]

One of H.M.'s letters read,

> I am surely glad to learn you are planning to write your doctor's dissertation on this subject. If I can be of any help in this, please let me know. I believe I mentioned to you that I am trying to write a book on the subject. Perhaps we can be of mutual help to each other from time to time.[12]

The seeds of a very important relationship were planted in those few exchanges.

The Morris family went through many changes during their six years in the Deep South. The physical environment was pleasant and interesting, but the spiritual environment brought challenges. The strong Catholic influence within the children's schools and neighborhood countered what the family taught at home. Drinking, profanity, and teenage rebellion were common. Peer pressure, both from within and outside the church, became a concern, especially for Henry III.

With two pre-teens and three small children, Mary Louise began a child evangelism class in their home that usually in-

H.M. and family (left); Mary Louise holding Rebecca (right)

cluded about 20 neighborhood children. She was hostess and teacher most of that time.

Henry III and Kathy both subscribed to the Bible Memory Association. Each week they learned and quoted 25 verses, which allowed them to earn credit to go to a Christian camp. John and Andy both decided to follow Christ and were baptized during these years.

Their sixth and last child was born in Lafayette two years after they arrived. Because of the Catholic opposition and threats to the family, there was some concern about Mary Louise being entrusted to the Catholic hospital. The family prayed a good deal for this situation, and God answered. On December 19, 1953, Rebecca Jean was born, attended to by a kind and efficient staff.

Mary, Henry III, Rebecca, and Andy in 1953

The house the family rented belonged to an elderly Cajun gentleman named Mr. Guidry. He lived in a garage apartment behind the house, with close relatives on either side. He and his family could be quite cross with the very active family that lived between them. Mary Louise was perpetually concerned about her brood's rowdy behavior, and, of course, rumors and tall tales blossomed among the children of scrapes with the scary neighbors. However, the Lord gave grace in this uncomfortable situation, and the children soon learned respect for the neighbors and their property.

Robert Lee Morris with Mamie and their children

There were changes to the extended family as well. Mamie, the faithful grandmother who led H.M. to the Lord as a child, passed away soon after they arrived in Louisiana. Her death, though difficult for H.M., provided an opportunity for him to share the gospel with the family, and it seemed to have a real impact. Over the course of several years, H.M.'s uncles Robert and Gordon decided to follow Christ, partly due to Mamie's testimony and partly as the result of H.M.'s book, which he had shared with them. H.M. learned from his uncles that his grandfather, Robert Lee Morris, accepted Christ two weeks before he died, no doubt because of the prayers of his wife, Mamie.

Henry Senior

In 1953, H.M. learned that his father, Henry Senior, had given up drinking and joined a Baptist church in Houston. Henry Senior visited the family often in Lafayette and was especially pleased with H.M.'s books, giving many away to friends. H.M. was convinced his father was a genuine believer. This was a timely answer to prayer, because on Christmas Day 1955, his father was found alone in his apartment, dead of an apparent heart attack at age 62.

Because of their proximity to Houston, the family maintained closer contacts with their relatives. H.M.'s mother, Ida, and his brother Dick and wife Helen were maturing as believers. Now there were cousins to visit. H.M. was grateful that his whole family seemed to be turning to God.

During their six years in Louisiana, H.M. and his family witnessed many evidences of the Lord's blessing on their work and testimony, both professional and spiritual. Nevertheless, they began to sense God leading them to another field.

The school achieved accreditation, but the possibility of a graduate and research program seemed remote. H.M. felt he needed credentials in recognized university research to be an effective leader among Christians in the field of creationism, and the professional challenge at Southwestern seemed to be over.

However, the most compelling indication it was time to move was the urgent need to take their children to a community with a good church and Christian friends. Their oldest was soon to enter high school, and the pressure from unbelieving peers was becoming treacherous.

For these and other reasons, H.M. and Mary Louise began to knock on some doors and test the waters to see if God was leading them in another direction. They applied for several foreign engineering positions, still wondering if God might allow them to be missionaries. The Israeli Institute of Technology in Haifa was searching for a professor of hydraulic engineering, as was the Poona University in Bombay, India. In both cases, H.M. was tentatively appointed to the position, pending government clearance. But once these schools realized his strong

H.M. and family

Christian position, they rejected him. H.M. later recalled how
he felt at the time:

> I still knew deep in my heart that the greatest need
> of all in the Christian world was for a return to sol-
> id Biblical Christianity here in America, which of
> course had become the base of world missions. Evan-
> gelism and missions in themselves, vital as they are,
> could be only superficial and ephemeral without a
> solid foundation of truth in doctrine. And the rea-
> son for such widespread departure from the faith was
> the undermining and near-destruction of the foun-
> dation of all foundations—namely, the doctrine of
> the transcendent Creator and His special creation of
> all things. This was the greatest need, and also the
> special work God had prepared me for. This became
> more and more obvious.[13]

Eventually, H.M. received an offer from Southern Illinois
University. The university had started a two-year pre-engineer-
ing program and desired to upgrade this into a full College of
Engineering. They wanted H.M. to design the four-year program, including courses, facilities, equipment, and faculty. He
would become the first Dean of Engineering if the state legislation approved the new college.

H.M. asked the university for a higher salary. They agreed,
and H.M. interpreted this, along with the exciting professional
opportunity, as evidence of the Lord's leading.

In many ways, they hated to leave Southwestern Louisiana
Institute and Lafayette. Their work there was fruitful and the
blessings abundant. The students and faculty all came to appreciate H.M.'s character and professionalism, and the Gideons
valued his leadership. One of his students wrote a letter that

best expresses his reputation and hard-earned legacy in Lafayette.

Dear Dr. Morris,

One of the most satisfying experiences in my life has been this brief association with you. From it I have drawn inspiration and a strengthening of faith....Because of your faith and shining example, many have turned to Christ for the first time. Others have begun a critical, soul-searching evaluation of their purpose in life, realizing that something was missing.... Perhaps this statement by one of your students will express all that I have attempted to say. We were discussing various subjects, including goals in life, families, moral virtues, etc., when he suddenly said, "You know, a fellow couldn't do better than to model his life on Dr. Morris's."

God's purpose in sending you here is manifest in all your works. May you derive the strength and wisdom to fulfill His purpose in your new mission. To that end I will remember you in my prayers.

Sincerely, Mark[14]

11

From the Valley
to the Mountains

In Christmastime of 1956, the Morrises waved goodbye to Lafayette and headed north to Southern Illinois University at Carbondale, Illinois. The warmth and charm of the Deep South was replaced by the chill of an Illinois winter. Carbondale was a coal and railroad town near the Illinois coal fields and on the main line of the Illinois Central Railroad.

To the young family now accustomed to bayou country, the rolling, tree-covered hills of southern Illinois were breathtakingly beautiful, but the town seemed less than impressive,

and the campus was uninviting to its new professor. It was once a teachers' college and had a handful of old buildings, a few new ones, and many wooden temporary ones. Yet, since becoming a university, its student population mushroomed, and the administration expressed big plans for expansion, including a future college of engineering.

The winter that year was colder than usual, with much snow, sleet, and ice. The small house the Morris family rented was old and heated by a coal furnace, requiring a new routine—ordering coal, loading the stoker, removing the clinkers and ashes, and carrying them deep into the woods. The furnace and duct system proved inefficient, and on particularly cold days family members took turns standing over the register just above the furnace. Tending to colds, earaches, chicken pox, tonsillitis, and mumps consumed much of Mary Louise's time, between shuttling the healthy children to their various schools. Most days, H.M. walked the mile to campus over paths treacherous with ice. His health also suffered. A bad infection blocked his ears, and he was practically deaf for almost a month.

Then came spring—and tornado season. Southern Illinois lies in Tornado Alley, and it seemed to the family like they spent half their time huddled in the southwest corner of the basement, waiting for the tornado alert to be withdrawn. The storms did little damage to their neighborhood, but several tornadoes skipped directly over the house.

The Morrises joined University Baptist Church soon after arriving in Carbondale. It was a typical Southern Baptist Church conveniently located three blocks up the street. However, outside of church services there was little Christian fellowship—no Gideon camp, Christian school, or InterVarsity Christian Fellowship. H.M. recalled later:

The Morris children (left); Rebecca and Mary (right)

One main purpose I had in wanting to leave Lafayette was to find a better spiritual environment for the children, but this was hardly realized in Carbondale. There was not quite as much drinking and immorality around them, but the church and schools were no better. Henry [III] and Kathy were in the university-sponsored school which had a highly-trained faculty and excellent facilities. It was a "progressive" and humanistically-oriented school, however, and seemed to be no better, if as good, in actually teaching them anything of value.[1]

Even so, the children found some interesting activities. Henry III joined an organization called the Sea Scouts. John and Andy played Little League baseball. Kathy continued piano lessons, and John began to play the violin. The two youngest played in the coal bin—to their mother's distress.

The university turned out to be a tremendous disappointment for H.M. He had been intrigued by the challenge of organizing and heading a new engineering school. But as he became involved in laying out curricula, budgets, and lab facilities, he realized that the administration was not going to invest much serious support, either financially or promotionally, to produce a high-quality engineering college.

The Illinois legislature planned to vote in the spring on whether to approve the engineering school for Southern Illinois University, so H.M. needed to prepare a well-organized proposal. Consequently, he traveled to many other engineering

Mary Louise and H.M.

schools to compare and plan. Most private schools were very helpful, but the University of Illinois at Urbana—the only other state engineering school—was strongly opposed, fearing competition for state funds.

Mary Louise with the children

In mid-spring, the depressing news came that the legislature did not approve the Southern Illinois University engineering school. H.M. had come to Illinois because of the strong assurance that he would be dean of an engineering college. That prospect now seemed far in the future. H.M. reflected:

> Consequently, I finally had to decide it had been a mistake for me to come to Southern Illinois University in the first place, my motives having been primarily financial and professional rather than spiritual. Now both the spiritual and professional aspects of the job seemed minimal and the good salary was certainly not an adequate reason in itself for staying. I therefore began to pray seriously about leaving, but wanted to be as sure as possible of the Lord's leading this time.[2]

In his search for alternative employment, several possibilities emerged. A position at the University of Arizona appeared ideal. After attending the convention of the American Society of Engineering Education, he found openings at Colorado State University and the University of Buffalo, another in Pennsylvania, and one in Tennessee. The Ohio University at Athens and the one in Pennsylvania offered H.M. positions, but a chance meeting with a faculty colleague from Minnesota turned out to be a divine appointment. This friend, Russ Brinker, had recently resigned as Chairman of Civil Engineering at the prestigious Virginia Polytechnic Institute.

Just a few days after returning from the convention, H.M. received a phone call from the Dean of Engineering at Virginia Polytechnic Institute. Russ had recommended him for the position of Civil Engineering Department head, and the faculty wanted him to come to Blacksburg for an interview.

The train trip to Virginia passed through the heart of the Appalachian Mountains. H.M. watched out the window with awe as the train slowly wound through the tree-covered hills. The countryside was as beautiful as any he'd ever seen, and the plateau between the Allegheny and Blue Ridge Mountains where Blacksburg, Virginia, lay was breathtaking.

Three faculty members met him at the Christiansburg train station. They were Christians and seemed genuinely anxious for him to come. The dean was gracious and friendly, as were all the civil engineering staff members—even after H.M. explained his beliefs in special creation and the Genesis Flood. They had already reviewed his credentials, recommendations, and books, and proceeded to give him a formal offer for the position.

Dr. H.M. Morris

H.M. felt that these circumstances were favorable, and it appeared the Lord was leading him to take the offer, but even so, he and the family spent several days praying before he accepted it. He would not make a hasty decision again.

Finally confident that the Lord had made His will known, they packed up again after school was completed and headed for Blacksburg, Virginia. Highway 460 seemed the shortest route but turned out to be the slowest, with innumerable mountains to cross, slow curves, and switchbacks in and out of the hollows. Like most families, the combination of small children, crowded car, and endless winding had a predictable outcome, and they were forced to stop frequently along the way. Even so, the mountain communities and landscapes captivated them, creating a lasting memory.

12

Letting Go

At Virginia Polytechnic Institute, H.M. reached the height of his professional engineering career. In 1957, VPI was one of the largest engineering schools in the country and much more highly rated than Southwestern Louisiana Institute. It had a strong graduate program and was one of only 30 that could award a Ph.D. in civil engineering. Four hundred students pursued degrees in the civil engineering department, 20 of whom were studying on the graduate level. H.M. was appointed head of the department, and the school was enthusiastically supporting growth and research. It appeared to be an excellent environment for professional progress, and H.M. was thrilled to be back in graduate work and research.

The town of Blacksburg was small but quaint, with a population of less than 10,000, and had a strange blend of cultures. The college community of intellectuals and liberals lived alongside the backwoods Appalachian culture—with very little in-between. Blacksburg was definitely off the beaten track, yet those who lived there loved its beauty and isolation. H.M. wrote his relatives of its charm:

Virginia Polytechnic Institute

Blacksburg is located on a plateau at 2100 feet eleva-
tion, above the surrounding valleys. You don't actually realize you're in the mountains as long as you're
in the town, but just outside the town limits, you
start to go down and you can look across the valleys toward the adjacent mountains. The mountains
and hills are covered with trees and grasses that give
a deep blue-green hue to everything, in patterns that
are often fantastically beautiful. I've been in some 26
states now, but have never seen any country as beautiful as around here.[1]

H.M. was encouraged that the college already had an active InterVarsity Christian Fellowship organization on campus.
There was also a Baptist Student Union chapter, and he immediately got involved with both. But finding a good church
proved difficult since the Baptist church was quite liberal in
doctrine and compromising in its stand on biblical inerrancy.
However, it was the best option for appropriate children's activities, and within a few months the family joined. By October
1957, H.M. was teaching the college Sunday school class and
Mary Louise was teaching junior girls.

John, Andy, Mary, and Rebecca (left); the
Morris home in Virginia (right)

Feeling content they would stay for many years, H.M. applied for a loan and bought a new house that had enough space for his family. It was difficult financially, but the house had a large basement, two small bedrooms, and even an extra room for an office. The property backed up to a farm and was situated on a hill that overlooked the beautiful valleys beyond. In fact, according to the local engineers, the house sat exactly on the continental divide. Rain on one side flowed west into the New River and eventually into the Gulf of Mexico. On the other side, the water filled the tributaries that entered the North Fork Roanoke River on its way to the Atlantic.

Morris family at Christmas

With two teenagers, H.M. and Mary Louise quickly realized the need for good influences from Christian friends and activities. The churches in both Lafayette and Carbondale did not provide either fellowship or spiritual training. Unfortunately, the Baptist church in Blacksburg followed the same trend. Consequently, they decided to form a Youth for Christ club. For a few years, the group met in their home and provided support, but it could not take the place of a good church. The familiar pattern of teenage rebellion soon emerged, the all-too-common result of negative peer pressure set against high family standards. Both strong-willed teens reached for their independence. Their eldest son, Henry III, soon joined the Army and was confronted with the consequences of rebellion; the daughter progressed with intense determination to become a missionary. These familiar family struggles and blessings repeated throughout their years in Virginia.

Mary Louise with the children

Having experienced such tremendous growth and fellowship through the Gideon ministry, H.M. immediately hoped to repeat that blessing in Blacksburg. There was no established Gideon camp, but there were several Gideon members who were willing to work toward that end. They began a Sunday weekly prayer breakfast and soon grew to become one of the most active camps in Virginia. Blacksburg offered a much more receptive environment than Lafayette, and testaments were distributed to the schools, motels, and hospitals of the area. They also held monthly services at various prison farms, with several hundred men making professions of faith over the years.

The Gideons

In terms of professional development, these years were the most fruitful in H.M.'s engineering career. His success as an administrator, author, and professor was reflected in various Who's Who publications and professional societies.

Dr. H.M. Morris

Upon arrival at Virginia Polytechnic Institute, he began adding hydraulics courses to the curriculum, just as he did at Southwestern Louisiana Institute. He "made some statistical analyses to show that hydraulic engineering played a much larger part in the career of the average civil engineer than most colleges apparently realized."[2] These studies were eventually published in the *Journal of Engineering Education.*

There were no good textbooks in hydraulic engineering for these courses, so H.M. developed a detailed set of notes for class handouts. This involved much research, and H.M. consequently became an active member in the hydraulics division of the American Society for Engineering Education, serving as chairman of the Committee on Applied Hydraulics for three years. Eventually these class notes accumulated, and he compiled them into a full-fledged textbook. H.M. submitted this to various publishers, and practically all wanted to print it. No comparable textbook for that specific field

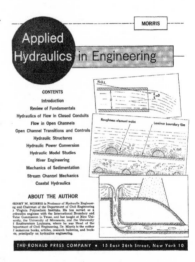

of engineering was available. Ronald Press finally published it in 1963 under the title *Applied Hydraulics in Engineering.* It was quickly adopted as the textbook in almost every university that offered hydraulic courses.

Gradually, as head of the department, he reorganized and developed the engineering program, until eventually there were over 20 full-time, highly qualified faculty members. They received maximum ratings in two accreditation inspections and

Professor H.M. Morris

gained approval to offer a Ph.D. program. With a new building and hydraulic lab facilities, sponsored research contracts
increased and enrollment grew to about 600 in 1969. H.M.
noted, "The faculty and graduate students were producing
much excellent research, with many good papers published in
top-notch professional journals. The spirit was excellent among
both students and faculty."[3]

H.M. received a number of professional honors and rec-
ognitions during this time. He was promoted to Fellow in the
American Society of Civil Engineers and in the American Association for Advancement of Science—the highest and most
coveted status in both. He was elected Secretary-Editor of the
Civil Engineering Division of the American Society for Engineering Education and appointed to the accreditation committee of Engineers Council for Professional Development.
He earned other grants and positions as well. Of this, H.M.
admitted:

> All of these attainments and honors were much more
> an indication of the Lord's blessing than of my abili-
> ties. Although I enjoyed research and teaching in hy-
> draulics, this was still only the means to an end. My
> real interests were in the Lord's work, but I realized

that I would have to maintain almost impeccable academic credentials in order to maintain an effective Christian witness in the world of science and education. I really believe it was because I did try to put the Lord first in all things and to maintain an uncompromising testimony for Christ, especially including the foundational truth of special creation, that God so blessed my rather ordinary talents and efforts in engineering.[4]

Although the Gideon ministry blessed him personally and his professional career continued to progress, H.M. still felt a growing conviction that the most strategic contribution he might make in the Christian world was to cultivate the message of genuine biblical creationism. It seemed that almost the whole evangelical community had surrendered to evolutionism and uniformitarianism. Uniformitarianism claimed that all natural processes functioned in the same ways in the past as they do in the present, and these processes could be used to explain the origin and development of everything. Closely tied to evolutionism, it led to denials of the global Flood and supernatural creation.

Those Christians who tried to reconcile creation with the eons of time assumed by evolutionists held to the compromising day-age and gap theories. But both were unscriptural and unscientific. Their straining of the foundational chapters of the Bible was invariably undermining the gospel, the deity of Christ, and His substitutionary atonement. H.M. reflected:

It had become clear—at least to me, to John Whitcomb and a few others—that the real key to a revival of creationism on both a Biblical and a scientific basis, was the restoration of the Genesis flood to its

rightful historical status as a global hydraulic cata-
clysm that had completely altered the surface of the
earth, as well as its demographics, its meteorology, its
ecology and most other aspects of its natural systems.
As the Bible says: "The waters prevailed exceedingly
upon the earth" (Genesis 7:19).[5]

From his earliest interest in creationism, H.M. tried to develop a definitive treatment of this subject. His graduate work
was geared toward it, he wrote various papers for publication,
and an expansive manuscript was growing. As his knowledge
and research developed, it became clear to him that it was
impossible to harmonize the inerrant biblical record with the
evolutionary-uniformitarian system of Earth history. The fossil
record and the sedimentary rocks could, and should, be rein-
terpreted in terms of the hydraulic effects of the Flood.

Certainly, he was not the first to advocate Flood-interpret-
ed geology. He wrote:

> In fact most of the "founding fathers" of the science
> of geology had been flood geologists. Many profound
> books had been written on this theme by great scien-
> tists back in the 17th, 18th, and 19th centuries. Isaac
> Newton himself was a believer in flood geology, along
> with many other great men of the time. However…
> the latter half of the 19th century saw the capitu-
> lation of practically the entire scientific, education
> and religious establishments to evolutionary unifor-
> mitarianism….Only a handful of more-or-less fringe
> scientists and theologians…continued to believe in
> recent creation and flood geology. The most effective
> of these had been an Adventist writer, George Mc-
> Cready Price….It was his textbook, *The New Geology*,

which had been most influential in my own scientific thinking about the Flood.[6]

H.M.'s friend Dr. John Whitcomb, a formidable Bible scholar, was also working on a manuscript developed from his Th.D. dissertation on the global Flood of Genesis. Through their correspondence, they assisted and encouraged each other, eventually determining that a combined text of theology and science would be the most effective. Both realized the strategic importance of such a book and sensed the guiding of the Holy Spirit.

Dr. John Whitcomb

H.M. in Pittsburgh in 1959

But the research and collaboration to produce what became *The Genesis Flood* proved to be a rigorous and lengthy process. The deeper H.M. researched, the more problems required solutions, which in turn generated more research. "I clearly had the sense of God's guidance, spending considerable time in prayer, and then frequently finding solutions to problems that at first seemed almost insurmountable."[7]

They planned to publish the book in 1959 since that was the Darwinian centennial year. In January 1959, H.M. sent the manuscript to the publisher for review. It had become much longer than previously agreed upon. In addition, many key scientists, geologists, and theologians were asked to review the manuscript, and the remainder of the year was spent in making revisions. By November 1959, the book was still unfinished and had 540 pages, 22 pages of bibliography, and 400 references.

By the following March, the publisher had the finished manuscript. In July, Dr. Whitcomb and H.M. met in Winona Lake, Indiana, the home of Grace Seminary, for a final review.

The Whitcomb family in 1960

During the meeting, *The Genesis Flood* almost met a substantial setback. H.M. brought his family along on a vacation while he attended an engineering meeting at the University of Michigan. His daughter Kathy had spent the summer working at the Winona Lake Bible Conference, and he planned to pick her up on the way and also spend some productive hours with Dr. Whitcomb. The two families met for a picnic at the lake. While the children were splashing around and playing, the men sat in lawn chairs with the manuscript between them. The wind suddenly picked up, and the manuscript pages for *The Genesis Flood* scattered across the beach. Screaming and laughing, the children managed—with dirty and wet hands—to collect all the pages and prevent it from being hopelessly damaged.

In August, the galley proofs were finally at the printers, but the indexes needed to be prepared—no easy task for such a lengthy book. It took months. Not until February 1961 was the book printed and ready for distribution.

Morris family at Winona Lake

Several publishers hesitated to take on the project because of the controversy it was certain to generate. One of the reviewers of the manuscript, Rousas Rushdoony, a prolific author himself, was enthusiastic and recommended Hayes Craig and his Presbyterian and Reformed Publishing Company. Mr. Craig agreed to publish the book and produced a promotional brochure listing the contents and many testimonies of scientists who had read it.

An Unusual and Important New Book
THE GENESIS FLOOD
The Biblical Record and its Scientific Implications

THE GENESIS FLOOD presents a new and powerful system for unifying and correlating scientific data bearing on the earth's early history. Frankly recognizing the inadequacies of uniformitarianism and evolutionism as unifying principles, the authors propose a Biblically-based system of creationism and catastrophism. They stress the philosophic and scientific necessity of the doctrine of "creation of apparent age," as well as the importance of terrestrial history of geologic and hydrologic "catastrophes," especially that of the great Deluge inscribed in the records of the Bible and in the legends of early peoples all over the world. The book is careful and courteous in its treatment of opposing viewpoints, and is thoroughly documented and up-to-date.[8]

Dr. H.M. Morris (left); Dr. John C. Whitcomb (right)

The brochure also included the reviews of 30 scholars who read the manuscript, generating a great deal of interest.

Merrill F. Unger served as the Professor of Old Testament Studies at Dallas Theological Seminary. He said:

> A stimulating and accurate exposition of what the Bible says about the Noahic Flood, a brilliant and compelling challenge to the theories of modern uniformitarian geology, and a desperately needed discussion on a crucial point of the alleged clash between Scripture and Science.

A.G. Tilney, Hon. Secretary of the Evolution Protest Movement of England, said:

> We feel bound to agree with the publishers that this *Genesis Flood* may well prove to be one of the most widely-discussed and possibly one of the most significant books of our times. Readers in search of information will be sure to find this book a mine with many veins, while those of fixed ideas—yet who are honest enough to read it—will find it a minefield dangerous to prejudice. A new era of faith in the truth of the Word and the Works of God, past and to come, may result from a full and fair study of *The Genesis Flood*, for which we are most grateful.

George McCready Price authored many works on the Bible and science. He said:

> In my judgment, this is the most noteworthy volume on Christian apologetics in years. Since admission in favor of the truth from the ranks of its enemies constitute the strongest kind of evidence, it is surely no small feat of scholarship to assemble some 2000

statements from over 600 modern scientific writers in support of the many detailed specifications in these early chapters of Genesis, with most of these scientific statements being not more than five years old.[9]

Even with limited advertisement, *The Genesis Flood* quickly attracted attention. Book reviews appeared in newspapers, magazines, and journals in rapid succession. All were either very favorable or highly critical—none were neutral.

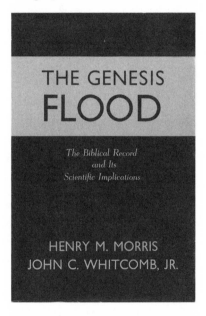

The negative reviews came from neo-evangelical organizations such as the American Scientific Affiliation, InterVarsity, Wheaton College, and *Eternity* magazine. Critics found geological points to criticize but utterly ignored the main point of the book. The authors emphasized over and over again that the geological explanations were tentative and much research was needed to restructure the geological data within the biblical framework, but that these questions could not be allowed to bring the authority and clarity of Scripture into question.[10] The book demonstrated that the Bible could not be reconciled with a local or tranquil flood. None of the reviews questioned the biblical exposition—they simply ignored it. They rejected Flood geology and disregarded Scripture while still protesting they believed the Bible.

However, the great majority of reviews were favorable. The fortuitous combination of a faithful theologian and a godly professional scientist sparked a sense of urgency in many Christians—they began to recognize the reliability of the Bible in matters of science.

Many scientists, preachers, and people of all walks of life enthusiastically endorsed the book, and the modern creationist revival began to take shape. Some even reported that they were led to follow Christ after reading it. Many were thrilled at the suggestion that Christians need not be intimidated by unifor-mitarian dogma. A reawakening to the reliability of the Bible unfolded for thousands of Christians.

Over the next few years, more than 40 published book reviews came out in magazines, journals, and quarterlies. *The Genesis Flood* was included in *Eternity's* "Most Significant Books of 1961." The 1962 February issue of *United Evangelical Action* listed it in the "25 Best Books of 1961," and it was one of the "Choice Evangelical Books of 1961" published by *Christianity Today*. Quite a few realized that this book just might be a turning point for many Christians:

Robert K. DeVries of Dallas Theological Seminary said:

To my way of thinking, this is the most significant book on science and Scripture which has been published by an evangelical in the past 25 years.

J. G. Vos, Editor of *Blue Banner Faith and Life*, said:

> The publication of *The Genesis Flood*, the reviewer dares to predict, is likely to cause some scientific climbing down. Scientific journals will probably pass it by with haughty disdain…but truth is extremely stubborn and persistent, and though crushed to earth will rise again….Let us await with interest the reaction to this book in scientific (and theological) circles of our own day….Sooner or later they will have to take notice of it and evaluate the arguments presented by its learned authors.

Rabbi Lawrence Duff-Forbes published a review in *Israel's Anchorage*:

> This book is more than timely; it is overdue….It will challenge any who have bowed in submission to uniformitarianism and will stimulate, encourage, and equip the increasing number of those whose faith and intelligence combine to prefer the lofty sanity of biblical statement rather than the ever-accumulating and highly-conflicting evolutionary hypotheses. This book may well serve as a fulcrum to pry loose from its established bedding the currently accepted tables of alleged geological ages.[11]

Publication of *The Genesis Flood* significantly impacted H.M.'s personal life and schedule. He began to receive many invitations to speak from all over the country. He had traveled quite a bit before, but the opportunities increased tremendously as churches, schools, science organizations, and conferences requested his presence to expound on and defend his position.

The book provoked intense interest from scientists, both

Christian and secular. Many were hostile to this attack on their comfortable uniformitarian beliefs, but others expressed genuine openness to frank discussions of the scientific data presented in the book. The consequences of acceptance were enormous for those working in related fields such as geology, paleontology, and even biology.

For years, H.M. accepted as many invitations as possible, feeling certain that this was the task God had assigned him. It was not a job he relished because he did not enjoy traveling or speaking. Public appearances were difficult for him. From childhood, he had been introverted and shy, with a tendency to spend his time reading, away from the emotional hazards of a social life. Even at this time in his life, he preferred research and writing but felt keenly that the message of creationism must be presented to all who would listen.

Although H.M. regretted that his extensive travel did not allow for much family time, he worked hard to make certain his time at home was spent with eternal values in mind. His spiritual influence was most strongly felt around the table. With few exceptions, the family ate morning and evening meals together. Someone always read a passage from the Bible, and they took turns praying. None of his children forgot the sound of his voice as he read the Bible, never faltering or stumbling over words or inflection. His familiarity with each chapter was so intimate it seemed he must have practiced and memorized each line. His awe of Scripture left an indelible mark on each child's heart.

Because his travel expenses were usually paid, he was able to include the family in some wonderful vacations around the United States. They visited Lake Ontario, the Catskills, the Grand Canyon, Washington D.C., the Rockies, Yellowstone,

Morris family in New Mexico (left); visiting Williamsburg (right)

Williamsburg, Disneyland, Pensacola, Niagara Falls, and many other exciting places.

Although H.M. needed to spend his spare time preparing to speak, the family devoted the hours of car travel to singing and games. The children demanded over and over that he sing his favorite cowboy songs, vestiges of the dreams of his boyhood. "Empty Saddles in the Old Corral" and "Tumblin' Tumbleweeds" were his specialties, along with songs of cattle roundups and hard gallops across the deserts of West Texas. Hours of the game Stinky Pinky challenged the kids as well. It involved asking a question whose answer must be in the form of a rhyme. What is a small boxer? A lighter fighter. The teens were expected to play "Stinkity Pinkity," which involved at least a three-syllable answer like "president's residence."

In spite of these opportunities, his speaking and travel took its toll. With the absence of a dependable church, the limited family times, and the pressure of peers, they experienced the difficulties that often come to families involved in ministry.

In an effort to fill one void, H.M. and Mary Louise felt led to follow the New Testament example of a "church in the house" (1 Corinthians 16:19). They were members of the Baptist church, but the liberal leanings were discouraging, and opposition was surfacing to H.M.'s teachings on creation and the reliability of the Bible. When *The Genesis Flood* was published, the pastor reacted very negatively, refusing even to read it because it questioned "science." So, the small nucleus of the DeBusk and the Morris families determined to meet for fellowship, and they eventually organized the College Baptist Church in August 1961. Two pastors from nearby towns, Rev. James Comstock and Pastor Leonard Routh, were concerned about the lack of a fundamental church in Blacksburg and offered to help with the preaching. It was a difficult beginning. They faced much opposition from the established churches, but it was refreshing to finally have a place where college students and families could hear the Word taught as inspired truth.

For a while, the church held services in the National Guard Armory, which required much cleanup and setup work. Soon the church meetings were moved to the basement of the DeBusk home, with Sunday school classes in various bedrooms. Gradually, new families joined, as well as many students from both

Foreign engineering students at VPI

College Baptist Church

Navigators and InterVarsity groups at Virginia Polytechnic Institute. H.M. became involved with many foreign students in the engineering department, and some of these also came to Christ and attended services at College Baptist Church.

Through the following years, College Baptist suffered frequent setbacks because of the unusual town's environment, and they met both internal and external hindrances. However, the church stayed firm to its commitment to the Word of God and its love for Christ. It was led by very capable and faithful pastors, eventually merging with another group and taking on the name Harvest Baptist Church. For H.M. and Mary Louise and the other founders, it served a vital function for their children. Many of its young members went on to work in full-time ministry, firmly committed to the inerrant Word of God.

As interest in *The Genesis Flood* grew and H.M.'s national renown became undeniable, the administration at Virginia Polytechnic Institute raised objections to the unwanted publicity. A new university president took over, established a more liberal administration, and even eliminated the required military corps. This destroyed a century-long tradition and substantially changed the university's image of patriotism and political conservatism. It became obvious to H.M. that the new leaders did not appreciate being associated with a religious fundamentalist, even though they could not fault him for his thriving engineering department. Consequently, achieving the goals for his department became an uphill battle against administrative opposition.

H.M. later recalled:

> [The Dean] called me in and told me, in effect that I should "cool it" as far as my writing and speaking on creationism were concerned. He indicated that, on at least two occasions, [the president] had been petitioned by faculty delegations to get rid of me, but [the president] had not acceded to their request. I surmised that these faculty members were probably from the Departments of Biology and Geology, since they complained that I was "embarrassing" them nationally, and thus tarnishing VPI's image. This was a veiled threat that, if I did not stop what I was doing, [the president] might not be so solicitous of my "academic freedom" next time around. I replied, of course, that I was always careful to distinguish my own views from any official VPI position, and that I was not neglecting any academic responsibilities to my department, so that I saw no reason why I should not continue to exercise my academic freedom in this way. He could not find anything specific to criticize or refute, but it was obvious that the pressure was increasing. In any case, I certainly did not intend to yield to such threats.[12]

Once again, H.M. wondered if the Lord was leading him to another assignment. He began to earnestly pray for guidance and knock on other academic doors. The University of New Mexico and Auburn University in Alabama seemed particularly favorable, and a number of Christian colleges urged him to consider joining their faculty. H.M. and Mary Louise prayed seriously about each offer but sensed the Lord was not leading to any of these.

Dr. H.M. Morris and Dr. Bob Jones

During this period of uncertainty at Virginia Polytechnic Institute for H.M., the Lord used *The Genesis Flood* as a catalyst to begin the modern creationist revival. Most theologians and evangelical scientists of the day who took a stand against evolution still almost invariably accepted the geological age system and thus had to advocate either a local or tranquil flood and the day-age or gap theory. For this reason, most Christians majored on evangelism and "spirituality," leaving the natural sciences to the secularists, liberals, and humanists. However, apparently many people more or less secretly believed in a recent creation but had been hesitant to take a public stand. These were awakening in increasing numbers to openly endorse creationism.

Several champions of the faith who were also scientists recognized the beginnings of this awakening. They determined to organize, share ideas, and research some of the unresolved questions in creationism. Walter Lammerts, Will Tinkle, John Klotz, Wilbert Rusch, Paul Zimmerman, Frank Marsh, John Grebe, Edwin Monsma, David Warriner, Karl Linsenmann, Willis Webb, Tom Barnes, Clifford Burdick, Harold Slusher, and Duane Gish were just some of the other men who took on this mission. All were firmly committed to an inerrant Bible and recent creation.[13]

These scientists, along with H.M., organized the Creation Research Society in 1963, with 18 serving on the board of directors. Membership grew rapidly, and by the first year included almost 100 people. Each voting member was required to have at least a master's degree in a field of natural or applied science and had to sign the statement of faith. By the summer of 1964, they published the first *Creation Research Society Quarterly*. The depth of the articles improved with each issue, quickly surpassing the American Scientific Affiliation journal in biblical integrity and scientific quality. Dr. Walter Lammerts served as president of the society for its first four years. H.M. was elected president in 1968, serving for five years. By 1973, membership had increased to 412 voting members and probably three times that many subscribing members.

The Creation Research Society filled a great need in the Christian community, and its influence was widely felt. H.M. wrote, "To the frequent claim that 'all scientists are evolutionists,' one could now document the fact that many scientists were now creationists."[14]

However, to the Virginia Polytechnic Institute administration, these creationist developments were an annoyance, and in spring 1969 they decreed that H.M. would no longer be the Civil Engineering Department Head. This was unexpected and sudden. The Civil Engineering Department was thriving, and there were no faculty or student complaints, but the decision was irrevocable. The administration expected him to resign rather than accept the demotion. Instead, H.M. proposed a sabbatical year that would give him time to update and enlarge his hydraulic engineering textbook, with the agreement that he would resign the following year. It was an unprecedented proposal, but to his surprise the university accepted, undoubtedly anticipating the uproar from the engineering department members, who appreciated his leadership. H.M. recognized the hand of God in this arrangement and accepted it as an answer to prayer.

By the end of the year, the administration had changed, the textbook was revised, his replacement was installed, and the situation was such that the engineering faculty urged him to stay. He would have an ideal position—a high-salaried, tenured, full professorship. He could forgo the administrative headaches and have the freedom to plan and pursue his own

Andy, Ida, and John Morris

program. It also seemed that the young and struggling College Baptist Church still needed them. And with two children in college and their youngest daughter a sophomore in high school, a move would be difficult, both financially and emotionally. There were many sensible reasons to stay at Blacksburg.

Nevertheless, H.M.'s conviction grew that the Lord was leading him out of engineering and toward a full-time Christian ministry. He increasingly sensed the urgent need for some kind of creationist educational center where research could be conducted and textbooks produced. Ideally, this would be in connection with a Christian college. He began inquiring with various Christian schools, hoping to generate interest in a center for creation studies on an established campus.

The only one interested appeared to be LeTourneau College in Texas, which was the only Christian college that offered an engineering degree. They offered him the position of Dean of Engineering. H.M. agreed to go there but only if the offer included the position of director for a new creation studies center. After some months of consideration, the LeTourneau administration determined that such a venture would be too costly and too controversial.

Firmly convinced that this was the work to which he was called, H.M. finally acknowledged that the only way to have a truly creationist school and research center would be to establish one himself. This would demand much personal and professional sacrifice, but his journey with the Lord had taught him that God's grace was sufficient for every task.

During these years in the pleasant hills of Virginia, H.M. was asked to relinquish much that he had worked so hard to

Mary Louise and H.M. in 1964 (left); Henry III and Rebecca in 1959 (right)

attain. Leaving Virginia Polytechnic Institute meant leaving his profession as an engineer to accept financial uncertainty and trust the Lord for the success of a fledgling ministry.

He also surrendered his eldest son to the Army at age 17 and another son to a worldly career in Los Angeles. He committed the protection of his eldest daughter to God when she headed as a single missionary to Wycliffe's jungle camp. Two other children were given over to the freedoms and responsibilities of a college campus. He had to release his wife to the will of the Father as she suffered the ravages of breast cancer. Through all these tests, he surrendered his own desires, and God proved faithful. Letting go of earthly attachments was the next step his spiritual journey required.

Having committed to completely surrender to the Lord's will, H.M. traveled to the Torrey Conference at Biola College in January 1970 for a divinely appointed meeting with Dr. Tim LaHaye. Consequently, and after much prayer, he made the life-changing decision that took him to San Diego, California, to start a new ministry...one that required his full commitment for the rest of his life.

13

Deep Wounds

H.M. likely wrestled with the costs of his calling as he left his profitable career in Virginia to start a new phase in his ministry. Years before, he read a tract by G.D. Watson titled "Others May, You Cannot!" He understood then and throughout his life that compromise must never characterize his Christian faith. He treasured the thoughts in this essay, particularly over the next few years of struggle and frustration, and shared it often with family and friends. (See Appendix E.)

H.M. began a new chapter of life in January 1970 at the annual R.A. Torrey Bible Conference at Biola College, named in honor of the school's first dean. Fifty years earlier this great evangelist took the infant H.M. in his arms and petitioned God's blessing on his life. Now a prepared and courageous defender of the faith, the now-grown H.M.

Dr. H.M. Morris

R.A. Torrey Bible Conference

stood at the crossroads ready to launch a ministry that would one day provide hundreds of thousands of Christians with the weapons they needed to engage the enemy.

In spite of his introverted nature, H.M. always seemed to be involved in starting things. He instinctively saw needs and moved to fill them. He helped form three InterVarsity chapters, two Gideon camps, a church, and the Creation Research Society, in the face of obvious opposition. But the most "impossible" undertaking took place in San Diego.

In California he joined Drs. Tim LaHaye and Art Peters, pastor and associate pastor of Scott Memorial Baptist Church. These two men hoped to start a Bible college modeled after Bob Jones University, their alma mater. Dr. LaHaye was well known for his books, but neither pastor had experience in education or in developing plans for curriculum or faculty.

In his search for a location to organize a creation center, H.M. had become disillusioned not only with secular universities but Christian schools as well. "The monstrous evolutionist-humanist delusion"[1] controlled the textbooks and influenced

Dr. Tim LaHaye and Dr. H.M. Morris

the ideologies at all levels of Christian education. Many evangelical colleges compromised their stand, and even colleges that were creationist avoided the controversy and could not be counted on to take a strong position.

Dr. H.M. Morris and Dr. Jerry Falwell

The academic world needed something new.

He heard the concern from pastors, teachers, missionaries, and parents throughout his speaking travels. To H.M., the answer to the problem was a "true university system with undergraduate, graduate, and professional schools, with active research, extension, consulting and publishing programs as well. Such a center could take the lead in reclaiming science and education for Christ and then eventually the churches and the state as well."[2] Such a goal was idealistic, to be sure, but H.M.

181

felt the dominion mandate of Genesis 1:28 commanded believers to strive for just that. "The attitude of pietistic defeatism that had characterized evangelical Christianity for several generations"[3] in the scientific arena was damaging the spirit of the church.

Dr. H.M. Morris

His far-reaching goals struck a responsive chord with the two godly pastors from San Diego. Although their aim was just for a Bible college, they too recognized the need for something more. The theme song of Scott Memorial Baptist Church at that time was "Nothing Is Impossible When You Put Your Faith in God." Within a few months, this dynamic church embraced these new goals, and together Tim LaHaye, Art Peters, H.M., and the church family put plans into motion.

They named the new liberal arts school Christian Heritage College. Dr. Morris, as Vice President for Academic Affairs, was in charge of organizing the entire academic program. He also served as Director of the Creation Research Science Center, a research, writing, and teaching division dedicated to restructuring all fields of learning and practice in the integrating framework of creationism. Art Peters was Executive Vice President and Tim LaHaye the President. Kelly Segraves, the director of Bible-Science Radio, also joined the project and persuaded the others to include his organization within the research center. He took the position of Assistant Director.

Classes began in the fall of 1970 with a total of seven full-time students. H.M. taught two classes, Practical Christian Evidences and Scientific Creationism. These apologetics courses

Teachers workshop in 1972 (left); speaking to students (right)

were pioneering efforts and constituted the main distinctive of Christian Heritage College. The other classes were taught by very capable professors from within the church.

To his academic peers, the decision to leave Virginia Polytechnic Institute for this must have looked foolish. Even many of his Christian friends and members of the Creation Research Society thought it was a mistake. Nevertheless, H.M. moved forward, confident of the Lord's leading, and subsequent years revealed the tremendous impact that grew from this small beginning.

Christian Heritage College more than doubled in size each year for the next few years. Through the ministry of Tim LaHaye and H.M.'s lectures, students began coming from many different places. They constructed a new building on the church property in 1973 and upgraded the faculty yearly with qualified scientists such as Dr. Duane Gish. Dr. Harold Slusher joined the team and developed a new degree program in creationist-catastrophist geophysics. These and other blessings pointed to an exciting future. The college held its first com-

ICR at Christian Heritage College

ICR event

mencement in 1973, conferring degrees upon two graduates.

The most exciting development was the purchase of a 30-acre campus in El Cajon, a nearby community, with dormitories, dining hall, classrooms, library, athletic facilities, and a beautiful sanctuary. God provided the church and college an affordable situation with abundant room to grow.

H.M.'s workdays were filled with planning curricula and creating class notes, while most weekends were spent on the road speaking at churches, colleges, and conferences throughout the United States and beyond. Christians all over the world hungered for the truth of scientific creationism.

Encouraging events were occurring on the home front as well. His eldest son, Henry III, had been called by God after leaving the Army to study for the ministry. After several years at Bob Jones University, he took a pastoral position at a small church. He and his wife, Jan, came to California in 1975. Henry III finished his education at Christian Heritage and, at the insistence of Dr. LaHaye, became his father's office assistant.

H.M.'s eldest daughter, Kathleen, joined Wycliffe Bible Translators and married Les Bruce, a dedicated translator. They worked in New Guinea among the Alamblak tribe, striving to develop a written form of the language, teach them to read, and give them God's words in their native tongue.

Kathleen's house in New Guinea

H.M. and Mary Louise's third child, John, graduated from Virginia Polytechnic Institute and took an engineering job in Los Angeles. Through a renewed interest in creationism and a trip to the Holy Land with a Bible-science tour, he became convinced that he should get involved in the search for Noah's Ark. He re-

Dr. John Morris

signed his engineering job and went to work for Christian Heritage College as a recruiter and field scientist.

Andrew and Mary eventually joined the college staff after graduating from Bob Jones University, and Rebecca enrolled as a student at Christian Heritage. All of H.M.'s children were now walking with the Lord and serving their Creator.

However, trouble was brewing at Christian Heritage and the Science Center. Time and again, there were conflicts among the faculty, and H.M. worried that Christian Heritage College was drifting away from its original principles. The school was involved in the long process of obtaining accreditation, and some faculty resented the strong creationist stand and strict standards that hindered its acceptance. Other conflicts were related to particular biblical beliefs such as dispensationalism or Calvinism. Petty jealousies and trivial issues over leadership took their toll. The strained relationships filled H.M. with anguish, and he spent many hours on his knees pleading for the Spirit to intervene.

H.M.'s dream for the Creation Research Science Center was severely tested as well. At the beginning, and with serious reservations on the part of the three founders, the college board unwisely accepted eight members of Bible-Science Radio headed by Kelly Segrave as full members, joining Tim and Beverly LaHaye, Art Peters, and H.M. It wasn't long before these eight controlled the projects and decisions, and the leadership grew increasingly resentful of H.M.'s authority. An unexpected surprise came when Dr. Duane Gish contacted Creation Research Science Center, saying he felt the Lord was leading him to join the effort. Aware of Dr. Gish's outstanding credentials and breadth of knowledge in relevant sciences, H.M. was thrilled and accepted his application. He gave Dr. Gish the title Associate Director and naturally regarded him as second-in-command at the center. The resulting clash alerted H.M. to the extent of Kelly Segrave's ambition. Segrave and his supporting board members focused on political efforts, intending that H.M. serve merely as a figurehead with the Bible-Science group in control of the Creation Research Science Center.

Dr. Duane Gish (left); Dr. Gish and Dr. H.M. Morris (right)

Mary Louise and H.M.

By April 1972, the board, with its constitutionalized majority, voted 8-4 to separate from the college. They took the assets, the mailing list, and copyrights to all the textbooks that were written and published over the previous year and a half, and moved to another location. H.M., Dr. Gish, the LaHayes, Dr. Peters, and Dr. Slusher immediately resigned. Devastated by the seeming death of a vision, the faithful founders and their loyal staff met for prayer. Within a few days, they determined to reorganize, and the Institute for Creation Research was born.

Changes occurred rapidly as ICR got off the ground. The Creation Research Science Center advisory board, 12 scientists and theologians, elected to resign and join ICR as well. They established the ICR constitution to tie it to the college, and salaries were further reduced for a few months while college funds were used to support it. They started a monthly newsletter titled *Acts & Facts*, and a new mailing list began to grow. It was a financially difficult time for all involved, but they remained dedicated to their task. H.M. later recalled:

> This had been the culmination of a long-cherished dream, the beginning of a creationist liberal arts college, with a special creation studies division, commissioned to do research, writing, and extension teaching on creationism. Those plans had been complicated by the temporary attachment and subsequent de-

tachment of the Bible-Science Radio group from the organization, but the work continued essentially unchanged after the brief period of reorganization.[4]

Within a few months, the success of *Acts & Facts* encouraged many donors to get involved, and ICR became essentially self-supporting. New projects were started, and H.M., Dr. Gish, and Dr. Slusher wrote books and technical monographs. John Morris joined the staff and led an expedition to Mt. Ararat to search for Noah's Ark, the first of several trips sponsored by ICR. In the next few years, many talented scientists and researchers connected with ICR, either serving full-time or contracting for various college courses, special projects, or as speakers.

From the beginning, ICR tried to emphasize education rather than legislation as the best method for restoring creationism to its rightful place in the schools, the church, and the world. On the premise that the pen is mightier than the

Drs. Slusher, H.M. Morris, Gish, and J. Morris at ICR

sword, ICR developed its activities around literature, research, and teaching. H.M. felt that they could achieve the greatest impact by distributing quality publications at appropriate levels for students.[5] Accordingly, the ministry produced numerous books, pamphlets, articles, monographs, and textbooks. In fact, so many were written and publicized by associated creation scientists that H.M. and several others decided to start a publishing company dedicated to the creation and apologetics genre. Named Creation-Life Publishers, the company produced books on creation and the publications of Dr. LaHaye's Family-Life Seminars. It later became Master Books when it broadened its efforts to include other books and videos.

During his first decade at ICR, H.M. personally wrote five major books and co-authored several others with scientists and teachers. While at Virginia Polytechnic Institute, he wrote and published *The Twilight of Evolution; Science, Scripture, and Salvation; Biblical Cosmology;* and *The Bible Has the Answer.* In San

Dr. John Morris and the Ararat Team

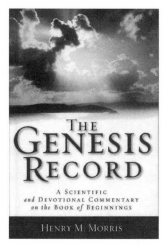

Diego, he added *The Remarkable Birth of Planet Earth*, an intro-
ductory treatment of creationism that was widely distributed
as a give-away through Jerry Falwell's Old-time Gospel Hour.
Many Infallible Proofs, Scientific Creationism, and *The Troubled
Waters of Evolution* were developed from his apologetics college
courses and published as textbooks. The book he enjoyed most
was his commentary titled *The Genesis Record*, an outgrowth of
class notes compiled from his senior Bible class. Another was
Education for the Real World, which Christian Heritage College
used as a statement of their educational philosophy. In 1977,
The Scientific Case for Creation was published. It contained no
biblical material, only well-documented information written
specifically for science-minded individuals.

In addition to education, ICR also emphasized research.
However, because of limited facilities and funds, they only initiated projects that didn't require laboratory facilities. Except
for the Ararat expeditions, most of these projects consisted of
geological field research or library and analytical research.

The teaching component of ICR developed into a number

of distinctive categories. All the scientists and teachers maintained full travel schedules, presenting creation seminars and conferences in cities all across the country. They frequently lectured in schools, colleges, and scientific organizations. Campus meetings were often sponsored by student Christian groups, but they always attracted many curious, yet skeptical, students and faculty. H.M. wrote:

> The most spectacular of these campus meetings by far have been the creation-evolution debates. These, more than any other one factor (except, perhaps, *The Genesis Flood*) brought the creationist movement to the attention of the scientific-educational community and excited the Christian community.[6]

H.M.'s first debate took place at the University of Missouri in Kansas City. He had never been in a debate and felt quite nervous, wondering what to expect. As it turned out, the evolutionist presented only the flimsiest of evidence and came unprepared to deal with the creationist arguments. The success of the debate stirred up tremendous interest, and the idea caught on nationwide. Soon student groups were inviting ICR scientists to their campuses for debates that drew overwhelming crowds. Dr. Duane Gish became extremely adept at debating and enjoyed the encounters. Dr. Morris was always somewhat reticent in this environment, having an intense aversion to arguing. He recalled:

> I have never gotten to where I enjoy the debates, and am always tense before and during the debates but I am not afraid of what I might encounter any more. We have debated many of the nation's leading evolutionary scientists and if there really were any good evidences for evolution or any real answers to the

creationist arguments, we would have heard them by now! The creationists almost invariably win the debate—not because we are good debaters but because the truth is on our side. Of course, no formal decisions are made as to the winner, but whenever there has been a student poll, this is always the result. Newspaper stories also seem nearly always to come to this conclusion.[7]

H.M. personally participated in about 30 debates, and altogether, ICR scientists participated in over 400 debates. This teaching ministry had a unique impact over the years on many campuses, with many dramatic results. Eventually, it became quite difficult to find qualified evolutionary scientists willing to debate.

ICR's Summer Institutes on Scientific Creationism were week-long, graduate-level courses with 30 hours of lecture, corresponding to two semester-hours of credit. They were held

Speaking in Turkey

at over 50 Christian colleges beginning in 1972 and provided another outlet for teaching ministry.

ICR experienced exhilarating growth in the '70s. God's hand was evident, and hundreds of thousands were exposed to the evidence for creation. For H.M., now in his 50s, the travel, speaking, writing, and planning were overwhelming yet thrilling. The message spread, and Christ was declared as Redeemer and Creator, encouraging thousands of disheartened believers.

His responsibilities were equally overwhelming at Christian Heritage College. The burden of dealing with faculty conflicts, curriculum development, and accreditation weighed heavily on him. The dream of a special graduate program in creationism, master's programs in Bible and Bible psychology, and other plans could not be launched until the school achieved accreditation, and the pressure to compromise was great. By the time he accepted the college presidency in 1979, the school had grown steadily and reached 500 students by 1980. Overloaded with administrative duties, for the first time in 37 years H.M. relinquished his classes. The demands of his position curtailed his writing time as well. Because of contro-

Dr. H.M. Morris (left); administration building at Christian Heritage College (right)

versy and compromise, prospects for his vision of a creationist university began to look dim.

A gulf developed between the goals of the college and ICR. Visits from the accreditation teams repeatedly blamed the school's strong emphasis on creation as the reason for rejection. The agency wouldn't allow them to pursue graduate programs, either, and it appeared that Christian Heritage College could more likely achieve accreditation if it were not associated with ICR. H.M. recalled:

> It seemed to me that the college, in order to achieve its overweening priority of accreditation, would very possibly either eventually decide to become a Bible college or else to compromise its position in the liberal arts area. Either situation would be disastrous to the ICR work if ICR were still a division of the college. Thus, contrary to my previous stand, I began to see that ICR would soon have to separate from the

Morris family in 1977

college if it were to remain viable and continue to grow in outreach and impact.[8]

The Lord's leading became clear. The responsibilities of administration in a growing college demanded H.M.'s full-time involvement. The rapid growth of ICR also demanded his full-time leadership. Even for an energetic and committed man, the demands were too great to accomplish both. H.M. realized his efforts should be focused on the tremendous potential of ICR. He should relinquish the burden of college administration to someone gifted for that service. Accordingly, he resigned as president of Christian Heritage College and began the process of separation.

The separation became official on February 1, 1981. The terms provided for mutual cooperation, shared staff, and shared facilities, and they benefitted both ICR and the college. Although H.M. continued to serve as Chairman of the Apologetics Department for two years, he was relieved to no longer be burdened with teaching and administrative responsibilities at the college.

Dr. H.M. Morris

However, his workload did not decrease. ICR's work expanded almost explosively. The demand for creationist literature was pressing. Churches and colleges clamored for ICR speakers. The Institute for Creation Research was gaining international attention—and opposition.

14
Bearing Much Fruit

H. M. had wanted to write even as a teen. Now he understood this was his calling. His heavenly Father developed in him a passion for sharing the message of the Creator and gave him the talent and desire to do the work. However, much of his writing was done in motels, airports, and airplanes because his numerous speaking engagements took him all over the world. When home in San Diego, his administrative duties left little spare time. Nevertheless, he always felt he should "redeem the time" (Ephesians 5:16), and so he wrote many of his books and articles by hand on a yellow notepad while waiting for a flight or resting in his motel room between speaking assignments.

During the next few years, he added several new creationist books to the list at ICR, including *Evolution in Turmoil*, *The Biblical Basis for Modern Science*, *The History of Modern*

Chinese seminary students at EMSI

Creationism, and *The God Who Is Real.* ICR published collections of his articles and those of other scientists as well.

His travels carried him to almost every U.S. state and many foreign lands, with Mary Louise usually accompanying him. Together they traveled to Canada, Hawaii, New Zealand, London, Australia, and other places around the world. One of the most unforgettable trips was to South Korea, where over two million Christians gathered for an outdoor Campus Crusade event. In the midst of rainy weather, H.M. and Mary Louise looked out over a sea of colorful umbrellas. Each one represented hearts hungry to hear God's truth. After an intensive speaking tour to many of the college campuses and churches in New Zealand, they visited their daughter

Tom and Libby Barnes, Mary Louise and H.M. Morris

Radio ministry

Kathy and son-in-law in New Guinea. For the first time, they saw their grandson Bobby, while staying in a stilt-supported, thatch-roofed house and getting acquainted with the primitive yet complex Alamblak people.

During the '70s, the last of H.M. and Mary Louise's children left home. Each married a mature Christian and established a family centered around Christ and firmly committed to the veracity of the Scriptures. Henry III and his wife Jan, John and his wife Dalta, Andrew, and Rebecca were all employed in various ways with ICR and Christian Heritage College. Mary Ruth married Paul Smith and spent years doing editorial work for H.M.'s many books. Rebecca married Don Barber, the director of Indian Hills Bible Camp. Grandchildren regularly visited their grandparents' home, bringing the familiar chaos and joy.

By 1980, the work at ICR was in full bloom. The science staff had grown considerably, and all scientists traveled extensively as the demand for creationist speakers intensified. A radio ministry supplied weekly creation programs for about 1,200 outlets nationwide, requiring professional recording. Research projects continued, while the staff also rolled out monthly articles, monographs, and books at a tremendous pace. They also held seminars, conferences, debates, children's classes, geology tours, TV interviews, and workshops. ICR rapidly became nationally and internationally known.

A proliferation of local, national, and international creationist organizations sprang up as a result of the huge interest in creationism. Hundreds of groups formed in North America, Europe, Asia, South America, Russia, and the Pacific, all with the goal of encouraging Christians and spreading the message of the reliability of

Mary Louise and H.M. with Schools for Christ and Paul Pang

Scripture. An eminent science historian at Wisconsin University, Dr. Ronald Numbers, noted:

> It is still too early to assess the full impact of the creationist revival sparked by Morris and Whitcomb, but it's to have been immense....Unlike the anti-evolution crusade of the 1920's, which remained confined mainly to North America, the revival of the 1960's rapidly spread overseas as American creationists and their books circled the globe....Creationism had become an international phenomenon.[1]

The news media everywhere featured articles on the subject and usually portrayed ICR as the "nerve center" of the creation movement. However, H.M. felt strongly that other creation groups were independently organized and must always remain autonomous. They should never be dominated by ICR or any other group. He believed that a true revival must begin in the hearts of individual Christians through the influence of the Holy Spirit, and not be the result of one book or one organization.

In 1979, H.M. got involved in another important development, the organization of the Transnational Association of Christian Schools (TRACS). He hoped it would become "a sort of international consortium of Christian schools of all types and levels, whose common bond is an educational system founded upon true Biblical Creationism and full Biblical authority in all courses, curricula and methods."[2] Accreditation had been a problem for Christian Heritage. H.M. believed TRACS could serve as an accrediting agency for Christian schools, eventually replacing the secular agencies that were so instrumental in causing Christian schools to compromise.[3] He dreamed that one day there would be a united Christian university made up of strong Bible-centered colleges from all parts of the world.

TRACS began with just a few prominent seminary and college presidents, including H.M. They carefully developed a well-structured accreditation system, and soon it became a significant force in education. In 1992, after a long struggle and much opposition, the U.S. Department of Education approved TRACS to be the official accrediting agency for Bible-centered creationist schools of all types and levels.[4] Today, over 60 colleges and seminaries have received accreditation through TRACS.

After separating from Christian Heritage College, the leadership at ICR began implementing the plan to establish their

Drs. H.M. Morris, John Morris, Duane Gish, Dick Bliss, Gary Parker, and Harold Slusher (left to right)

own graduate school. It kicked off the first year in the summer of 1981 with four master of science degree departments: biology headed by Gary Parker, geology by Steve Austin, science education with Dick Bliss, and astro/geophysics chaired by Harold Slusher. Tom Barnes served as the Dean. With 15 students enrolled by 1982, the ICR graduate school became an associate member of TRACS. By 1983, 50 students studied at various stages, with five completing requirements for their degrees.

To H.M., this development was of the utmost importance. He always believed the Christian world needed a place where science educators could increase their knowledge of science from a biblical perspective. Almost without exception, the sciences were taught in both secular and Christian schools with a backdrop of evolutionary dogma. If schools were to be reclaimed for the Creator, a significant body of teachers needed to be trained in scientific creationism. The ICR Graduate School was established to meet that need. Even if a master's degree from ICR held less weight than a similar degree from

Dr. C. Burdick teaching class at the ICR Graduate School

a university, it still made a huge difference in the hearts of students listening to a well-trained Christian science teacher. H.M. longed for a future where a Christian student could obtain a prestigious advanced science degree in an environment where his biblical worldview would not be repressed.

However, such a degree threatened the university system and its Darwinian adherents. Opposition over the next years was fierce. The California Department of Education initiated a campaign to stop the school. Years of court appearances and state appeals followed, but finally in 1992 the federal district judge ruled in ICR's favor. The official judicial declaratory judgment allowed not only ICR but all Christian schools the freedom

Dr. Duane Gish, Pastor Henry Morris III, and Dr. H.M. Morris

to teach their courses according to their own beliefs.[5]

In 1984, an ICR board member donated money to buy property in nearby Santee, California, to build a dedicated ICR facility there, complete with classroom, laboratory, library, office, and museum space. This allowed more video and audiotape production, along with increased research and publications. The daily devotional booklet *Days of Praise* was launched in 1985. H.M. wrote all of the devotionals the first year, with other writers contributing in later years. These free booklets attracted a tremendous number of subscribers, and the mailing list quickly grew.

ICR Dedication 1984: Gish, Morris, Jeremiah, and Whitcomb

ICR headquarters in Santee, California

Morris family At Wynola Bible Camp in 1987

H.M. carried a heavy workload for a man in his late 60s. Administrative duties for the extensive ICR ministries consumed much of his time, but writing articles and devotionals, editing, and speaking at various seminars demanded even more. He also took time to personally answer all the letters that came to him with questions concerning creation. Nevertheless, he managed to continue to write books, the one particular ministry that he felt was his life's calling. He hoped for the opportunity to retire so he could spend more time at this.

Fortunately, his son John, after receiving his Ph.D. in Geological Engineering, returned to ICR full-time and began to assist him. In 1985, the board appointed John Morris as Assistant Vice President to help with fundraising, editing, and correspondence. Three years later, having matured as a speaker, debater, writer, and leader, John assumed the position of Administrative Vice President in January 1988.

During this intensely busy season of his life, H.M. continued publishing books on creationism, such as *Creation and the Modern Christian*; *Science, Scripture and the Young Earth*; *Christian Education for the Real World*; and *Biblical Creationism*. But he found

Top: Andy, Henry III, and John
Bottom: Kathy, Rebecca, and Mary

greater satisfaction in writing commentary books resulting from his personal Bible study. He wrote *The Revelation Record* as a companion to *The Genesis Record*, and it was published in 1983. *Sampling the Psalms*, *The Remarkable Record of Job*, and *Creation and the Second Coming* also came out during this period, and *The Long War Against God* became a favorite among those interested in history.

ICR's ministry expanded even more in the '90s. With the extra space in Santee, they added an upgraded museum that greatly increased ICR's outreach. Hundreds of thousands of visitors came for the visual presentation of creation and Earth history. ICR's publications ranged from picture books for children to technical monographs for scientists. ICR constructed a new office building with technical studios and a large warehouse. Tours to the Grand Canyon, Mount St. Helens, Yellowstone, and Yosemite showcased many of the geological evidences for recent creation. Multitudes received ICR's *Acts & Facts* and *Days of Praise*. Many books were translated into other languages, and creationist organizations thrived in other lands.

The year 1995 marked a milestone in the history of the

Museum of Creation and Earth History
(above); Mary Louise and H.M. Morris,
Lolly and Duane Gish at Grand Canyon
(right)

modern creation movement. It
had been 25 years since ICR's
founding, and God greatly blessed the ministry during that time.
But much more work was needed. H.M.'s dream of a university
based entirely on the foundation of strict biblical creationism
was yet to be realized. The vision grew from his 35 years as a
Christian student, teacher, and administrator in schools dominated by evolutionary humanistic philosophy. He understood
that today's young people will be tomorrow's leaders, and there
was no more vital goal than to provide as many of them as
possible with a solid, biblical, Christian, creationist education.[6]

At 77, H.M. was approaching the end of his journey. At
ICR's 25th anniversary celebration in Washington, D.C., with

H.M. and Mary Louise 1990 (left); Drs. J. Whitcomb, J. Morris, and H.M. Morris (right)

Dr. Tim LaHaye as the special speaker, H.M. officially passed the mantle of leadership of ICR to his son John. An anniversary banquet was held later that fall in San Diego, with Dr. John Whitcomb as the speaker, to celebrate H.M.'s retirement. *The Defender's Study Bible*, a project H.M. worked on for several years, was dedicated and presented at both of those occasions.

Although his time as an administrator had passed, his ministry barely slowed. He continued to accept travel and speaking

Dr. H.M. Morris, President Emeritus (left); Morris family1983 (right)

assignments and wrote even more books. He continued at ICR as President Emeritus, now standing like Ezekiel's watchman on the wall (Ezekiel 3:17-19), gently warning those who would keep silent while unbelievers defiantly shook their fists at God and His Word.

15

The Last Mile

By God's grace, H.M. reached an advanced age. Old age brought wisdom and discernment, along with aches and pains and declining health. H.M. faced that greater burden with the expectation of a greater grace supplied by the One who faithfully provided for him throughout his life. With the worldwide recognition H.M. received, many of the opposition watched him, hoping to see him fall.

He encountered much heartache during this time. Andy was the fourth child of the family and did well in his career, graduating from Bob Jones University and assisting at Christian Heritage College as the head of the Business Administration Department. Ultimately, he received his Ph.D. in Information Management from Texas Tech. He and his wife, Rebecca, had three bright children

Andrew "Andy" Hunter Morris

and had moved to Tallahassee, Florida, where he held a faculty position at Florida State University. Early in 1989, Andy suddenly developed a fast-growing lymphoma, and in just a few short months passed into eternity. He was 39 years old.

Throughout the ordeal, his faith remained strong, and his confidence in his heavenly Father blessed all those who knew him and the thousands who read his printed testimony in ICR's *Acts & Facts*.

Andy and wife Rebecca

Many people shared H.M.'s anguish at the loss of his beloved son. On the very day Andy died H.M. was the commencement speaker at Liberty University. Two grandchildren, Henry IV and Scotta Morris, were graduating, and H.M. was to receive an honorary degree. He recalled about that day:

> Jerry Falwell asked me to lead in prayer....one of the hardest things I ever had to do, but the Lord enabled ....The Baccalaureate and awards ceremonies were very emotional, and I believe the Lord was honored.[1]

> As his father, I miss him very much, for he truly was a beloved son and I would willingly have died in his place, had it been possible. I begin now to understand something of Abraham's anguish when asked to offer up Isaac—or perhaps even a glimpse of the heavenly Father's agony of heart when He "spared not His own Son, but delivered Him up for us all" (Romans 8:32). That God gave His own Son to die for us surpasses all human comprehension, but He did! "What wondrous love is this, O my soul, O my soul!" Christianity and Christ are real indeed![2]

There were other personal stumbling stones along the way. His son John was diagnosed with multiple sclerosis. Then H.M. ran into financial concerns when a mudslide brought the hill

Drs. Falwell and Morris at Liberty University

behind their house into the back portion of their home, costing over $100,000 in repairs and hill reconstruction.

H.M. also began to experience health issues involving blood pressure, allergies, and problems with his feet. Three minor heart attacks caused by heart arrhythmia required hospital stays, and two more occurred that he chose to ignore. Laughingly, he often spoke of himself as the victim of the Second Law of Thermodynamics that he referred to in his messages.

Dr. John Morris

Even more serious issues plagued his wife, Mary Louise. A broken leg in 1999, high blood pressure, and congestive heart failure took turns breaking down her health. The most serious issue was the onset of Alzheimer's disease, which took her short-term memory.

Failing health and heartache did not lessen his determination to spend his remaining time in useful service for the Lord. There was even less time to waste. Throughout his life, a com-

Top: John, Rebecca, Mary, Kathleen, and Henry III
Bottom: Mary Louise and H.M. Morris

mand spoken by Jesus in a parable, "Occupy till I come" (Luke 19:13), was an overriding theme. He wrote:

> Right now, it is simply our responsibility to "occupy" until He comes. Each of us as a Christian believer has been given specific work to do under both the Dominion Mandate and the Missionary Mandate, so we need to be doing it, and doing it "with [our] might" (Ecclesiastes 9:10) as "to the Lord" (Colossians 3:23). "Whether therefore ye eat, or drink, or whatsoever ye do, do all to the glory of God" (1 Corinthians 10:31).[3]

At home or at the office, he continued to write, with beautiful handwriting, and always on a yellow pad. He produced another parade of books, including *Modern Creation Trilogy* (co-authored with his son John), *Their Words May be Used Against Them*, *Defending the Faith*, and *God and the Nations*. Commentary books included *The Remarkable Journey of Jonah*,

Treasures in the Psalms, *The Remarkable Wisdom of Solomon's Miracles*, and *For Time and Forever*. A collection of themed devotionals titled *Days to Remember* was published, and he also continued to write monthly articles and correspondence. By 2005, he had contributed 1,800 daily devotions to ICR's *Days of Praise*.

In 2005, H.M. knew the time for his ministry was drawing to a close. Yet, he prayed for the strength to finish one last task. The notes in his *Defender's Study Bible* needed to be updated and expanded. He worked as much as possible to complete the revision, but it was increasingly difficult.

His beloved wife, her memory gone, needed much care and attention. Family helped as much as possible, but with his failing health he knew he could no longer give her the care she deserved. Henry III, John, and Kathy all made arrangements in their homes and offered full-time care, but H.M. treasured his indepen-

Artist Mary Louise

dence. So, with the help of a live-in granddaughter and a hired nurse, he continued to live and work at his home. He was anxious to complete the notes for his *Defender's Study Bible* before it was too late.

At a family dinner party in January 2006 celebrating his and Mary Louise's 66th wedding anniversary, he announced he was sending Mary Louise for a "vacation" to Texas to stay with their daughter Kathy. After all, he said, "there are 66 books in

H.M., Mary Louise, 17 grandchildren, and some spouses

the Bible and this seems an appropriate time to...." No one wanted to finish that sentence. H.M. had always paid close attention to numbers and their significance. Just as the Bible was complete after 66 books, so their lives together were drawing to a close after 66 years of marriage.

Only two weeks later H.M. suffered his first stroke, leaving him unable to stand. Yet, his mind was as clear and focused as ever. Two weeks in a rehabilitation center offered a little more time to write one last book, *Some Call It Science: The Religion of Evolution.* His final thoughts on the great conflict of the ages between God and Satan were recorded with intensity, and he gave an impassioned warning to Christians.

> Just as pantheistic evolution served as the world's religion in the early days, so it may again in the last days. The New Age is really nothing but a revival in modern garb of the old age—that is, the first age after the Flood, when King Nimrod led the world in a united rebellion against the Creator....

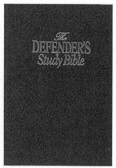

It is high time that people in general, and Bible-believing Christians in particular, recognize the foundational significance of special creation. Creation is not merely a religious doctrine of only peripheral importance, as many people (even many evangelical Christians) seem to assume. Rather, it is the basis of all true science, of true Americanism, and of true Christianity. Evolutionism, on the other hand, is actually pseudo-science masquerading as science. As such, it has been acclaimed as the scientific foundation of atheism, humanism, communism, fascism, imperialism, racism, laissez-faire capitalism, and a variety of cultic, ethnic and so-called liberal religions, by the respective founders and advocates of these systems. And now it is energizing the fearful New Age religions. The creation/evolution issue is, in a very real sense, the most fundamental issue of all.[4]

H.M. was almost giddy with anticipation. He knew the time was near, and he often said he was aching to see his Savior face to face. He wrote in one of his last books:

I hope that each reader will at least be a little better able to comprehend in some measure and appreci-

Mary Louise and H.M.

ate in greater measure this wonderful plan of God in creation. We do need to think way beyond our own little situation and our own personal salvation to see something of God's great plan for all of us in the ages to come. We must somehow learn to view things from His magnificent perspective, not just from our own very localized and limited point of view. His wonderful plan ranges all through time and all the endless ages to come. And—wonder of all wonders—we shall be there, too.[5]

In the closing days of February, he suffered a second stroke, leaving him unable to swallow and converse at length. His attention seemed to be drawn elsewhere, and his gaze seemed fixed on something far off. Yet, his mind was still keen, and he never lost his joy or sense of humor. Always the baseball fan, he joked, "Three strokes and you're out."

Dr. H.M. Morris

His daughter Mary arrived from Texas on February 25. He waited for her and then quietly asked for his briefcase. He pulled out his hospital bedside drawer, emptied it carefully into his briefcase, and set it aside. It was time to go. Nothing more needed to be said or done. Within minutes, he peacefully stepped from that vestibule of heaven into the very presence of God.

16

For Such a Time as This

God in His wisdom raised up a seemingly insignificant child from a broken home, protected him, and forged him into a weapon of great value for a specific battle. "For such a time as this," Dr. Henry M. Morris was born—a time when virtually the entire Christian world had surrendered to Satan's lies, denying the Creator's hand. He was destined and prepared for battle. Many turned to Christ for salvation through his witness. The faith of thousands more was strengthened or renewed. Numerous Christians had struggled with confusing messages and questioned the trustworthiness of Scripture. Their spirits welcomed the evidence and affirmation that Dr. Henry Morris taught. The Lord truly did allow this one faithful servant to change the world. God be praised for His glorious providence!

Epilogue

The ministry of ICR continued to grow through the years. Hundreds of thousands, probably millions, heard the message that God's Word is truth. On every page, and on every subject, God presented truth in simple, accurate, and, yes, scientific terms. The mission of ICR has not changed, nor have its tenets or standards.

John Morris continued as ICR's president for 10 years, but eventually the leadership of ICR passed to his brother Henry Morris III in 2005. Henry III, now prepared as a Bible scholar, and with an MBA from Pepperdine University, guided the ministry as CEO while John continued actively writing and speaking until his full retirement from ICR in 2014.

In search of a better economic and conservative climate, ICR moved its headquarters to Dallas, Texas, in 2006, which allowed ICR to expand its operations. Built on the guidelines of its founder, ICR's ministry continues to grow in research, writing, and education. Highly qualified scientists from many fields contribute excellent work, based on their intense research. ICR still encourages believers, engages the open-minded, and alarms the atheists.

Responding to contemporary expectations, new efforts were made to develop tools to challenge the next generation.

Stunning, theater-quality DVD series have been produced with viewer guides and student workbooks that have been used in hundreds of churches, large numbers of homeschool groups, and thousands of families. As the Lord provides, ICR plans to release more DVD series documenting the wonderful results of their research, another effective outlet for communicating the Bible's accuracy and authority

ICR's online graduate school shifted its emphasis to biblical apologetics and now enrolls more students than ever before. ICR plans to open a Discovery Center for Science and Earth History in Dallas, Texas. With an emphasis on discovering the truth, this modern visual presentation will reach thousands with the message that their Creator loves them and saves all who call on the name of Christ.

Building on founder Henry Morris' priceless legacy, ICR marches onward into battle with that same unshakeable commitment to the authority of God's Word. As long as God allows it, ICR will continue to expand its ministry, faithful to God in belief and practice—until Christ returns.

Appendix A:
Letters to H.M. included in
Defending the Faith

"I want to thank the Lord for the tremendous ministry you have had and are having. I have been a confirmed atheist and evolutionist, but the truth sets people free. It was because of one of Dr. Morris books that I accepted the Lord Jesus Christ as my personal Lord and Savior."

"I went to church up to the end of my teens and I then stopped. I considered myself a Christian, but accepted evolution as proved and tried to fit in what the Bible had to say with it, obviously with no success....I started to think about evolution and wonder how it worked. It made no sense to me. While I was doing this, I was looking at the books about the Bible in our central library. One of the books that caught my attention was *The Genesis Flood*. What you had to say made more sense to me than evolution ever did. I decided to look into it, and what I found absolutely appalled me. I decided to fight it at every opportunity I could get. It was this and a couple of other Christian books that the Lord used to lead me to himself, and I accepted Him as my Lord and Savior in 1983."

"Just a note to let you know that a fellow who attended a

creation lecture given by you and Dr. Gish in Oshkosh, Wisconsin, had his thinking regarding evolution shaken. He left the lecture with the conviction that Genesis is probably true and if Genesis is true, Revelation and the coming judgment are also. He acquired some Christian literature, read it, and accepted the Lord. He is now involved in full-time Christian service."

"This letter is nearly 20 years late....In many ways, *The Genesis Flood* was a turning point in my life. As a geologist...I was full of the textbook teaching....the absolute evolutionary emphasis taught in college and in graduate school. This had taken its toll....at that point I was introduced to *The Genesis Flood*. At last! Something that made sense! After that beginning, I read everything I could find on creationism and the ever-changing thoughts of the adherents of the evolutionary hoax....For the past several years I have been lecturing in creation and the various aspects of the creation/evolution debate to anyone who would listen....Thanks again for *The Genesis Flood* and all the books that followed; all have been used by God to profoundly affect many lives."

Appendix B:
Notes from Readers

Although Henry Morris stood on the shoulders of giants, he has himself become a giant in the world of science and Scripture. I have read many books, and his are among the most indispensable. —M. L. H.

I was introduced to books by Dr. Henry Morris, Jr., many years ago as an undergraduate at Bob Jones University, a school which had a very strong creationist point of view in its biology department. *The Twilight of Evolution* was required reading in one of my classes there.

Dr. Morris pioneered the field of flood geology in his great book, *The Genesis Flood*, with co-author John Whitcomb, after several generations had ditched biblical history as myth and superstition. Morris' death was a great loss to the creationist cause, but others…have picked up where Morris left off. My career after university took me into metals mining and the gas and oil fields. Although a creationist myself, I was frankly overwhelmed by the monolithic evolutionary dogma which controlled these fields, having had no academic training in geology. When confronted with "proof" that the earth was billions of years old all I could do was to mutter that I believed the Bible. As I have continued to read these creation scientists in my free time since college days, beginning with Morris, they have helped me to develop a scientific approach to geology which is in full accord with biblical teaching. Now I can look around myself and see evidence for the Genesis Flood everywhere. I can read a typical uniformitarian geology textbook and see inconsistencies and errors in the author's claims that evolution shaped the cosmos through deep time and I sometimes witness a geologist unwittingly admitting that only an incredibly great flood could possibly account for the land forms that we see everywhere. Because of the work begun by Morris I have full confidence in the truthfulness of the Bible in the face of the most stubborn "scientific" skeptics I have encountered. —T. B. (Comment posted on http://www.henrymorris3.com/icr-founder/)

Visited a good Creationist friend in IL back around 97 and he offered me a study Bible by Henry Morris for a very reasonable price...an invaluable resource that has strengthened my faith and emboldened me to answer the skeptics questioning and supposed contradictions of God's Word. I consider him a top apologist and [his passing] a real loss. —J. F.

I was converted at age 22. I believed Genesis but did not know how to reconcile it with science. Then I read *The Genesis Flood*....It has been a great blessing. —O. R. E.

By discovering his work on *The Genesis Flood* I could finally find God after years of being lost in the deep dark evil pits of atheistic evolutionary meaninglessness and deception. I keep doing what I can to serve Him right, even though I still often fail. —E. P.

My father used *The Genesis Flood* book by Dr. Henry Morris (hydrologist and author) in his research for a series of messages...when I was in high school.

That is when I first heard a lot about the physical power of the worldwide Flood of Noah's day! It contributed so much to geology and I have loved this subject, and all of apologetics, ever since. It played a BIG part in my attending Christian Heritage College in El Cajon, CA (now known as San Diego Christian College).

This is where I met my husband and made many life-long friends, as well as made a foundation for my life.

God's Word is full of true Science and Wisdom. I feel so privileged to have had Dr. Henry Morris as one of my professors and as a Chapel speaker while there.

He, along with Dr. John Morris, Dr. Duane Gish, Dr. Larry Vardiman and so many more are men that I treasure as men who love God and love real science. We are blessed to have lived in their time and to have learned from them! —J. D.

As a teenager, I would receive a take home paper to read, totaling four pages and folded down the middle like a newsletter. There was always a fiction story, a little Bible lesson and perhaps a puzzle or two. But what I looked forward to was the back page with an article by Mr. Morris. He explained fossils and dinosaurs....I will never forget those articles and was determined to find more articles written by him. God certainly honored my wishes and I now own the Henry Morris study Bible. —D. S. L. F.

While in Vietnam, someone very important to me was shot and killed. It broke my heart. I gave my life to Jesus Christ. I returned, paid my vows by doing a Catholic Novena, and started reading our Catholic Bible with notes. Then I got a Scofield Bible and thought it was great. Then I got a small illustrated booklet featuring Dr. Gish. My mind and heart went into overdrive. I got some Dr. Morris books, stayed in the fast lane, but settled down into cruise control. A tragedy was the occasion of my conversion, but a pioneering scholar and spiritual soldier was the means of my confidence. —M. L. H.

Appendix C:
A Parent's Prayer

I have a boy to bring up.

Help me to perform my task with wisdom and kindness and good cheer. Help me always see him clearly, as he is. Let not my pride in him hide his faults. Let not my fear for him magnify my doubts and fears, until I make him doubting and fearful in his turn.

Quicken my judgment so that I shall know to train him to think as a child, to be in all things pure and simple as a child.

I have a boy to bring up.

Give me great patience and a long memory. Let me remember the hard places in my own youth, so that I may help when I see him struggling as I struggled then.

Let me remember the things that made me glad, lest I, sweating in the toil and strain of life, forget that a little child's laughter is the light of life.

I have a boy to bring up.

Teach me that love that understandeth all things; the Love that knows no weakness, tolerates no selfishness. Keep me from weakening my son through granting him pleasures that end in pain, ease of body that must bring sickness of soul; a vision of life that must end in death. Grant that I love my son wisely and myself not at all.

I have a son to bring up.

Give him the values and beauty and just rewards of industry. Give him an understanding brain and hands that are cunning, to work out his happiness.

I have a boy to bring up.

Help me to send him into the world with a mission of service. Strengthen my mind and heart that I may teach him that he is his brother's keeper. Grant that he may serve those who know not the need of service, and not knowing, need it the most.

I have a boy to bring up.

So, guide and direct me that I may do this service to the glory of God, the service of my country, and to my son's happiness. Amen.

From Angelo Patri, A Parent's Prayer, The Scarsdale Inquirer, 5 (56): 4, December 20, 1924.

Appendix D:
God's Way of Salvation Tract

I. The Universal Fact of Sin

I Kings 8:46: "For there is no man that sinneth not."

Isaiah 53:6: "All we like sheep have gone astray; we have turned every one to his own way."

Romans 3:10, 12: "As it is written, There is none righteous, no, not one....They are all gone out of the way, they are together become unprofitable; there is none that doeth good, no, not one."

Romans 3:22-23: "For there is no difference: for all have sinned, and come short of the glory of God."

II. Physical and Spiritual Death the Penalty of Sin

Genesis 2:17: "But of the tree of the knowledge of good and evil, thou shalt not eat of it: for in the day that thou eatest thereof thou shalt surely die."

Romans 5:12: "Wherefore, as by one man sin entered into the

world, and death by sin; and so death passed upon all men, for that all have sinned."

Ezekiel 18:20: "The soul that sinneth, it shall die."

Romans 6:23: "For the wages of sin is death."

Hebrews 9:27: "It is appointed unto men once to die, but after this the judgment."

Revelation 21:8: "But the fearful, and unbelieving, and the abominable, and murderers, and whoremongers, and sorcerers, and idolaters, and all liars, shall have their part in the lake which burneth with fire and brimstone: which is the second death."

III. Sacrificial Death of Christ the Only Remedy

Romans 5:8: "But God commendeth His love toward us, in that, while we were yet sinners, Christ died for us."

Isaiah 53:4-5: "Surely He hath borne our griefs, and carried our sorrows. . . . But He was wounded for our transgressions, He was bruised for our iniquities: the chastisement of our peace was upon Him; and with His stripes we are healed."

1 Peter 2:24: "Who His own self bare our sins in His own body on the tree, that we, being dead to sins, should live unto righteousness: by whose stripes ye were healed."

Galatians 3:13: "Christ hath redeemed us from the curse of the law, being made a curse for us: for it is written, Cursed is every one that hangeth on a tree."

IV. Salvation the Free and Unmerited Gift of God

John 3:16: "For God so loved the world, that He gave His only begotten Son, that whosoever believeth in Him should not perish, but have everlasting life."

Romans 6:23: "The gift of God is eternal life through Jesus Christ our Lord."

Titus 3:5: "Not by works of righteousness which we have done, but according to His mercy He saved us, by the washing of regeneration, and renewing of the Holy Ghost."

V. Salvation Conditioned Only upon Personal Faith and Trust in Christ

Romans 10:9: "If thou shalt confess with thy mouth the Lord Jesus, and shalt believe in thine heart that God hath raised Him from the dead, thou shalt be saved."

Acts 16:31: "Believe on the Lord Jesus Christ, and thou shalt be saved, and thy house."

John 3:36: "He that believeth on the Son hath everlasting life: and he that believeth not the Son shall not see life; but the wrath of God abideth on him."

I John 5:12: "He that hath the Son hath life; and he that hath not the Son of God hath not life."

Acts 4:12: "Neither is there salvation in any other: for there is none other name under heaven given among men, whereby we must be saved."

Excuses and Objections Considered

I. Disbelief in the Bible

A. Most people will acknowledge the Bible to be one of the most marvelous of all books, even though they may not believe in its divine inspiration. But it is impossible to explain the tremendous moral and spiritual power of the Bible and its wonderful compilation and preservation if its writers were either deluded or deluders. Those who wrote the book believed and said that it and they were inspired by God. For example, note what the following said about their writings:

Moses: "Ye shall not add unto the word which I command you, neither shall ye diminish ought from it, that ye may keep the commandments of the LORD your God which I command you" (Deuteronomy 4:2).

David: "The Spirit of the LORD spake by me, and His word was in my tongue" (II Samuel 23:2).

Jeremiah: "Then the LORD put forth His hand, and touched my mouth. And the LORD said unto me, Behold, I have put my words in thy mouth" (Jeremiah 1:9).

Luke: "It seemed good to me also, having had perfect understanding of all things from the very first [literally, `from above'], to write unto thee in order, most excellent Theophilus" (Luke 1:3).

Paul: "But I certify you, brethren, that the gospel which was preached of me is not after man. For I neither received it of man, neither was I taught it, but by the revelation of Jesus Christ" (Galatians 1:11-12).

"Which things also we speak, not in the words which man's wisdom teacheth, but which the Holy Ghost teacheth" (I Corinthians 2:13).

Jesus Himself frequently quoted from the Old Testament as divinely authoritative. For example, see Luke 24:44:

"And He said unto them, These are the words which I spake unto you, while I was yet with you, that all things must be fulfilled, which were written in the law of Moses, and in the prophets, and in the psalms, concerning me."

Paul said: "All scripture is given by inspiration of God, and is profitable for doctrine, for reproof, for correction, for instruction in righteousness" (II Timothy 3:16).

Peter said: "For the prophecy came not in old time by the will of man: but holy men of God spake as they were moved by the Holy Ghost" (II Peter 1:21).

B. There is no proved fact of science or history that conflicts with any statement in the Bible. Furthermore, many discoveries of modern science have been hidden in the pages of the Bible for thousands of years. These include the roundness of the earth, the remarkable water cycle of meteorology, the rotation of the earth, the strong force of gravity, and many others. The theory of evolution (either cosmic or organic) has never been proved. Almost all the supposed evidences for it have, in recent years, been rejected even by many evolutionists. At the same time, evidence is multiplying that evolution on any large scale not only did not, but could not, take place.

C. There are hundreds of minutely fulfilled prophecies in the Scriptures, most of which have been proved to have been fulfilled long after being written. These prophecies include the history of such nations and cities as Egypt, Edom, Tyre, Sidon, Babylon, Persia, Syria, Greece, Rome, etc. The entire history of the Jewish land and people was foretold, to and beyond the present. Scores of prophecies of the first advent of Christ, including the date of His coming, His place of birth, His virgin birth, His ministry and miracles, His vicarious death, and resurrection, were given in the Old Testament. Many New Testament prophecies are being fulfilled today.

II. Belief that One's Personal Goodness Is Sufficient

A. God is perfectly righteous and just. Therefore, no one that is in any degree unrighteous or that comes short of perfection may be in fellowship with Him.

James 2:10: "For whosoever shall keep the whole law, and yet offend in one point, he is guilty of all."

Galatians 3:10: "For as many as are of the works of the law are under the curse: for it is written, Cursed is every one that continueth not in all things that are written in the book of the law to do them."

John 3:3: "Jesus answered and said unto him [Nicodemus, a very moral and even religious man], Verily, verily, I say unto thee, Except a man be born again, he cannot see the kingdom of God."

Galatians 2:16: "Knowing that a man is not justified by the works of the law, but by the faith of Jesus Christ, even we have believed in Jesus Christ, that we might be justified by the faith of Christ, and not by the works of the law: for by the works of the law shall no flesh be justified."

B. We can be brought into the fellowship of God only through the righteousness of Christ.

II Corinthians 5:21: "For [God] hath made Him to be sin for us, who knew no sin; that we might be made the righteousness of God in Him."

I Peter 3:18: "For Christ also hath once suffered for sins, the just for the unjust, that He might bring us to God."

III. Hypocrites in the Church

A. Most churches contain members who are themselves unsaved. This was true even of the very first Christian group. "Jesus answered them, Have not I chosen you twelve, and one of you is a devil?" (John 6:70). Even those who were believers were very imperfect at first. James and John were hot-tempered and self-seeking, Peter denied Christ, Thomas was a doubter, etc. This is true to some degree of all Christians, and Christians are commanded to "grow in grace, and in the knowledge of our Lord and Saviour Jesus Christ" (II Peter 3:18).

Real Christians do tend to develop a greater love for goodness and hatred for sin as they become older in the faith. "Therefore, if any man be in Christ, he is a new creature: old things are passed away; behold, all things are become new" (II Corinthians 5:17). Most will admit that, in general, real Christians live a more righteous and godly life than those who are unsaved. Moreover, a hypocrite is really nothing but a counterfeit Christian, and nothing is ever counterfeited unless it is itself of great value.

B. Regardless of the people in the church, each individual is responsible himself directly to God for his own sins, not those of someone else.

Romans 14:4: "Who art thou that judgest another man's servant? to his own master he standeth or falleth. Yea, he shall be holden up: for God is able to make him stand."

Romans 14:12: "So then every one of us shall give account of himself to God."

C. There is no other way provided for salvation except Christ, and each individual is responsible himself for accepting or rejecting Him.

John 14:6: "Jesus saith unto him, I am the way, the truth, and the life: no man cometh unto the Father, but by me."

Hebrews 2:2-3: "For if the word spoken by angels was stedfast, and every transgression and disobedience received a just recompense of reward; how shall we escape, if we neglect so great salvation; which at the first began to be spoken by the Lord, and was confirmed unto us by them that heard Him?"

IV. No "Feeling" or "Inner Compunction" to Accept Christ

A. Salvation depends only on faith, not on "feeling."

John 1:12: "But as many as received Him, to them gave He power to become the sons of God, even to them that believe on His name."

John 5:24: "He that heareth my word, and believeth on Him that sent me, hath everlasting life, and shall not come into condemnation; but is passed from death unto life."

B. A feeling of true peace, joy, and assurance of sins forgiven and everlasting life will be a result of faith, but cannot precede it.

Romans 8:16: "The Spirit itself beareth witness with our spirit, that we are the children of God."

I John 5:10-11: "He that believeth on the Son of God hath the witness in himself: he that believeth not God hath made Him a liar; because he believeth not the record that God gave of His Son. And this is the record, that God hath given to us eternal life, and this life is in His Son."

V. Unwillingness or Supposed Inability to Give up Sin to Live Christian Life

A. Salvation is a free gift and requires nothing in exchange, except to accept it gratefully and without reservation.

Ephesians 2:8-9: "For by grace are ye saved through faith; and that not of yourselves: it is the gift of God: not of works, lest any man should boast."

B. It is true that real Christians should and will seek righteousness because of the leading of the Spirit, and by virtue of their new natures. But God Himself will empower the believer to live the Christian life.

Romans 8:14: "For as many as are led by the Spirit of God, they are the sons of God."

I John 5:4: "For whatsoever is born of God overcometh the world: and this is the victory that overcometh the world, even our faith."

I Corinthians 10:13: "There hath no temptation taken you but such as is common to man: but God is faithful, who will not suffer you to be tempted above that ye are able; but will with the temptation also make a way to escape, that ye may be able to bear it."

Philippians 4:13: "I can do all things through Christ which strengtheneth me."

C. In any event, nothing is as important to give up as one's soul.

Matthew 16:26: "For what is a man profited, if he shall gain the whole world, and lose his own soul? Or what shall a man give in exchange for his soul?"

D. The Lord Jesus Christ gave up far more to save us than we ever will to accept Him.

II Corinthians 8:9: "For ye know the grace of our Lord Jesus Christ, that, though He was rich, yet for your sakes, He became poor, that ye through His poverty might be rich."

Philippians 2:5-8: "Let this mind be in you, which was also in Christ Jesus: who, being in the form of God, thought it not robbery to be equal with God: but made Himself of no reputation, and took upon Him the form of a servant, and was made in the likeness of men: and being found in fashion as a man,

He humbled Himself, and became obedient unto death, even the death of the cross."

E. A Christian gains infinitely more than he gives up.

Philippians 4:19: "But my God shall supply all your need according to His riches in glory by Christ Jesus."

I Corinthians 2:9: "But as it is written, Eye hath not seen, nor ear heard, neither have entered into the heart of man, the things which God hath prepared for them that love Him."

VI. Fear of Ridicule or Persecution

A. It is foolish to fear what men can do or say more than God.

John 12:43: "For they loved the praise of men more than the praise of God."

Proverbs 29:25: "The fear of man bringeth a snare: but whoso putteth his trust in the LORD shall be safe."

B. The Son of God endured ridicule and suffering for us.

Hebrews 12:3: "For consider Him that endured such contradiction of sinners against Himself, lest ye be wearied and faint in your minds."

C. It is a privilege, not a hardship, to suffer for Christ.

Matthew 11:6: "And blessed is he, whosoever shall not be offended in me."

Romans 8:17-18: "If so be that we suffer with Him, that we may be also glorified together. For I reckon that the sufferings of this present time are not worthy to be compared with the glory which shall be revealed in us."

I Peter 4:13-14: "Rejoice, inasmuch as ye are partakers of Christ's sufferings; that, when His glory shall be revealed, ye may be glad also with exceeding joy. If ye be reproached for the name of Christ, happy are ye; for the spirit of glory and of

God resteth upon you: on their part He is evil spoken of, but on your part He is glorified."

D. Realization of the full import of salvation emboldens the Christian.

Romans 1:16: "For I am not ashamed of the gospel of Christ: for it is the power of God unto salvation to every one that believeth."

VII. No Immediate Concern

A. Death and eventual judgment are certain. Therefore, God's offer of salvation should not be neglected or put off.

II Corinthians 6:2: "Behold, now is the accepted time; behold, now is the day of salvation."

Proverbs 27:1: "Boast not thyself of tomorrow; for thou knowest not what a day may bring forth."

B. The "unpardonable sin" of Matthew 12:31, is constant ignoring of the Holy Spirit as He seeks to lead the individual to accept Christ. This continual rejection of Christ finally results in such a hardening of the heart against Christ that acceptance is no longer possible and the person is completely lost.

Genesis 6:3: "And the LORD said, My spirit shall not always strive with man."

Hebrews 10:28-29: "He that despised Moses' law died without mercy under two or three witnesses: Of how much sorer punishment, suppose ye, shall he be thought worthy, who hath trodden under foot the Son of God, and hath counted the blood of the covenant, wherewith he was sanctified, an unholy thing, and hath done despite unto the Spirit of grace?"

Hebrews 10:31: "It is a fearful thing to fall into the hands of the living God."

Promised Blessings to the Christian

I. New Nature

II Peter 1:4: "Whereby are given unto us exceeding great and precious promises: that by these ye might be partakers of the divine nature, having escaped the corruption that is in the world through lust."

I Peter 1:23: "Being born again, not of corruptible seed, but of incorruptible, by the word of God, which liveth and abideth for ever."

II. Forgiveness of Sins

Ephesians 1:7: "In whom we have redemption through His blood, the forgiveness of sins, according to the riches of His grace."

I John 1:9: "If we confess our sins, He is faithful and just to forgive us our sins, and to cleanse us from all unrighteousness."

III. Holy Spirit

Romans 5:5: "And hope maketh not ashamed; because the love of God is shed abroad in our hearts by the Holy Ghost which is given unto us."

I Corinthians 3:16: "Know ye not that ye are the temple of God, and that the Spirit of God dwelleth in you?"

IV. Answered Prayer

I John 5:14-15: "And this is the confidence we have in Him, that, if we ask any thing according to His will, He heareth us: And if we know that He hear us, whatsoever we ask, we know that we have the petitions that we desired of Him."

Matthew 21:22: "And all things whatsoever ye shall ask in prayer, believing, ye shall receive."

V. Peace

Philippians 4:6-7: "Be careful for nothing; but in everything by prayer and supplication with thanksgiving let your requests be made known unto God. And the peace of God, which passeth all understanding, shall keep your hearts and minds through Christ Jesus."

VI. Comfort

I Peter 5:6-7: "Humble yourselves therefore under the mighty hand of God, that He may exalt you in due time: casting all your care upon Him; for He careth for you."

VII. Grace

II Corinthians 9:8: "And God is able to make all grace abound toward you; that ye, always having all sufficiency in all things, may abound to every good work."

VIII. Victory

II Corinthians 2:14: "Now thanks be unto God, which always causeth us to triumph in Christ, and maketh manifest the savor of His knowledge by us in every place."

IX. God's Presence and Guidance

Hebrews 13:5: "Let your conversation be without covetousness; and be content with such things as ye have: for He hath said, I will never leave thee, nor forsake thee."

X. Resurrection and Glorification at Christ's Return

Philippians 3:20-21: "For our [citizenship] is in heaven; from whence also we look for the Savior, the Lord Jesus Christ: who shall change our vile body, that it may be fashioned like unto His glorious body."

I Corinthians 15:22-23: "For as in Adam all die, even so in Christ shall all be made alive. But every man in his own order: Christ the firstfruits; afterward they that are Christ's at His coming."

XI. Eternal Life and Happiness with Him

I Peter 1:3-5: "Blessed be the God and Father of our Lord Jesus Christ, which according to His abundant mercy hath begotten us again unto a lively hope by the resurrection of Jesus Christ from the dead, to an inheritance incorruptible, and undefiled, and that fadeth not away, reserved in heaven for you, who are kept by the power of God through faith unto salvation ready to be revealed in the last time."

If you have not yet accepted the Lord Jesus Christ as your Personal Saviour, there is no adequate reason why you should not do so, and every reason why you should. So believe in Him and receive Him TODAY—NOW!

A printable version of this tract is available at ICR.org/store.

Appendix E:
Others May, You Cannot!

If God has called you to be really like Jesus, He will draw you into a life of crucifixion and humility, and put upon you such demands of obedience, that you will not be able to follow other people, or measure yourself by other Christians, and in many ways He will seem to let other good people do things which He will not let you do.

Other Christians and ministers, who seem very religious and useful, may push themselves, pull wires, and work schemes to carry out their plans, but you cannot do it, and if you attempt it, you will meet with such failure and rebuke from the Lord as to make you sorely penitent.

Others may boast of themselves, of their work, of their successes, of their writings, but the Holy Spirit will not allow you to do any such thing, and if you begin it, He will lead you into some deep mortification that will make you despise yourself and all your good works.

Others may be allowed to succeed in making money, or may have a legacy left to them, but it is likely God will keep you poor, because He wants you to have something far better than gold, namely, a helpless dependence upon Him, that He may have the privilege of supplying your needs day by day out of an unseen treasure.

The Lord may let others be honored and put forward, and keep you hidden in obscurity, because He wants to produce some choice fragrant fruit for His coming glory, which can only be produced in the shade. He may let others be great, but keep you small. He may let others do a work for Him and get the credit for it, but He will make you work and toil on without knowing how much you are doing; and then to make your work still more precious, He may let others get credit for the work which you have done, and thus make your reward ten times greater when Jesus comes.

The Holy Spirit will put a strict watch over you, with a jealous love, and will rebuke you for little words and feelings, or for wasting your time, which other Christians never feel distressed over. So make up your mind that God is an infinite Sovereign, and has a right to do as He pleases with His own. He may not explain to you a thousand things which puzzle your reason in His dealings with you, but if you absolutely sell yourself to be His love slave, He will wrap you up in a jealous love, and bestow upon you many blessings which come only to those who are in the inner circle.

Settle it forever, then, that you are to deal directly with the Holy Spirit, and that He is to have the privilege of tying your tongue, or chaining your hand, or closing your eyes, in ways that He does not seem to use with others. Now, when you are so possessed with the Living God that you are, in your secret heart pleased and delighted over this peculiar, personal, private, jealous guardianship and management of the Holy Spirit over your life, you will have found the vestibule of Heaven.

From George Douglas Watson, "Others May, You Cannot," public domain.

Appendix F:
H.M.'s Handwritten Testimony

Like most people in the South, and especially Texas (!) I was brought up under religious influences, going to Sunday School regularly every week and even sometimes staying for church. My grandmother often talked to me about the Lord and I recall being somewhat alarmed at her prediction of the end of the world, which evidently some evangelist had scheduled for 1933. ~~When I recall at the time our events~~ When I was eight years old, my mother gave me a Bible. I began reading it, at Genesis, perhaps not the best place to start, but nevertheless this was the Word of God and God spoke to me through it. I don't remember much about it – that was a long time ago! – but somehow in the process I became convinced that I personally needed a Saviour, and, the best I understood, trusted the Lord Jesus to forgive my sins. I was baptized and, for a while, had a real consciousness of the presence and power of the Lord in my life.

But then we moved to a different city and a different church, the depression came, and things began to get rough! My parents were divorced about then and my mother had to support my two younger brothers and myself. But in spite of real poverty, living in a broken home, the influence of friends who were anything but Christian, and my own indifference to the Lord, He still remained faithful.

All through high school and college, I continued to be religious on Sunday morning and go my own way the rest of the time. The combined influence of evolutionary teaching ~~in college~~ and "devil-utionary" living in college just about erased any resemblance to ~~state~~ genuine Christianity in my life. Nevertheless, I continued to believe in Christ and can remember nightly asking Him to help me overcome the ungodly practices in my life – profanity, especially – as well as the spiritual cowardice that made me ashamed of being thought religious and prudish.

After graduation ~~and searching~~, I took a job as a government engineer, by divine coincidence in the city ~~Los Angeles~~ where I had lived as a small boy, and started going again to the church of my grandmother. The pastor was a faithful preacher of the Bible and of the Lord Jesus Christ, and I began to think again along lines that had long been dim in my mind. More importantly I began again to read the Bible, and God always uses His Word when a person reads with a desire to know more about Him.

Many things happened that the Lord used. I was married then, and my wife - whose spiritual background was of about the same calibre as mine though in a different denomination - and I both began to study the Bible and to grow together in the Lord desiring our home to be built on Him. I joined the Gideons about then, - and this fellowship of actively Christian laymen has also been a great blessing.

But there was still something missing. I could not recall any exact time or place or conversion "experience," still ~~had afer too many times I had~~ spent far too much time in wilful interests of my own, ignoring God's will, and consequently often would experience times of doubting whether or not I had ever really trusted Christ as Lord and Saviour, - whether, as the Bible puts it, He had really "saved" me. Because to be saved means not only to be saved from the punishment of sin in hell. The Bible says that the Lord Jesus is "able to save unto the uttermost them that come unto God by Him."

Three years after graduation I was called back to teach in my alma mater. I really felt God leading in this decision and now keenly felt the responsibility of helping these students who were spiritually drifting just as I had been. But still there was little power and much defeat and doubt in my life, and I certainly could never help anybody much under these conditions.

One day I locked my office door, knelt by my desk and had it out with the Lord. I told Him that, as best I understood, I believed that His Son, Jesus Christ, had died for me, to take away my sins, and that I wanted to live for Him alone. I asked Him to give me real assurance of salvation and to fill my life with the Holy Spirit, and then to use me however He would.

God graciously answered that prayer, as of course He had promised to do, all along. Since then, there have been many times of difficulty, but never of doubt - many times of failure on my part but none on His!

Notes

Prologue
1. John Morris, 2006, pamphlet on the life of Henry M. Morris.

Chapter 1
1. Roger Martin, 1976, *R.A. Torrey: Apostle of Certainty*, Murfreesboro, TN: Sword of the Lord Publishers, 277.
2. R.A. Torrey, 2004, *How to Pray & How to Study the Bible*, Peabody, MA: Hendrickson Publishers, 7.

Chapter 2
1. Henry M. Morris, circa 1980, "The Peace of Our Children," unpublished manuscript, 6.
2. Henry M. Morris, 1997, "Contending for the Faith," unpublished manuscript, 2.
3. Henry M. Morris, *The Western Forum of the First Baptist Church, El Paso, TX*, VII (20), May 22, 1930.
4. Morris, "Contending for the Faith," 3.
5. Ibid.

Chapter 3
1. Henry M. Morris, circa 1980, "The Peace of Our Children," unpublished manuscript, 15.
2. Ibid, 30-31.
3. Henry M. Morris, 1997, "Contending for the Faith," unpublished manuscript, 8.
4. Ibid, 11.

Chapter 4
1. Henry M. Morris, 1997, "Contending for the Faith," unpublished manuscript, 15.
2. Ibid, 14.
3. Ibid, 18.
4. Ibid, 15.
5. Ibid, 15.
6. Ibid, 16.

Chapter 5
1. Henry M. Morris, 1997, "Contending for the Faith," unpublished manuscript, 22.
2. Ibid, 23.
3. Ibid, 24.
4. Ibid, 25.

5. Ibid, 20.
6. Henry M. Morris, letter dated October 22, 1939.
7. Morris, "Contending for the Faith," 27.

Chapter 6
1. Henry M. Morris, circa 1980, "The Peace of Our Children," unpublished manuscript, 81-82.
2. Henry M. Morris, 1997, "Contending for the Faith," unpublished manuscript, 31.
3. Ibid.
4. Ibid.
5. Ibid, 34.
6. Morris, "The Peace of Our Children," 152.
7. Henry M. Morris, letter dated May 22, 1942.
8. Henry M. Morris, letter dated February 8, 1942.

Chapter 7
1. U.S. official document.

Chapter 8
1. Henry M. Morris, 1997, "Contending for the Faith," unpublished manuscript, 43.
2. Henry M. Morris, letter dated January 1, 1945.
3. Morris, "Contending for the Faith," 41.
4. Ibid.
5. Ibid, 42.
6. Ibid.
7. Henry M. Morris, letter dated April 7, 1943.
8. Henry M. Morris, letter dated April 22, 1944.
9. Morris, "Contending for the Faith," 50.
10. Henry M. Morris, letter dated July 1, 1946.

Chapter 9
1. Henry M. Morris, 1997, "Contending for the Faith," unpublished manuscript, 51-52.
2. Morris, "Contending for the Faith," 57.
3. Ibid, 63-64.
4. Ibid, 64.
5. Ibid.
6. Ben F. Allen, letter dated December 12, 1948.
7. Molleurus Couperus, letter dated March 16, 1947.
8. Wilbur Smith, letter dated January 17, 1947.
9. Arthur I. Brown, letter dated May 8, 1947.
10. J. Oliver Buswell, letter dated September 10, 1946.
11. Morris, "Contending for the Faith," 63.
12. Ibid, 60.
13. Ibid, 66.

Chapter 10
1. Henry M. Morris, letter dated April 1, 1952.
2. Henry M. Morris, 1997, "Contending for the Faith," unpublished manuscript, 77.
3. Henry M. Morris, letter dated July 16, 1955.

4. Morris, "Contending for the Faith," 80.
5. Henry M. Morris, letter dated September 16, 1953.
6. Morris, "Contending for the Faith," 81.
7. Henry M. Morris, letter dated June 30, 1953.
8. Henry M. Morris, letter dated September 10, 1955.
9. John C. Whitcomb, letter dated September 20, 1953.
10. Henry M. Morris, letter dated September 22, 1953.
11. John C. Whitcomb, letter dated November 15, 1953.
12. Henry M. Morris, letter dated December 1953.
13. Morris, "Contending for the Faith," 83.
14. Letter dated December 19, 1956.

Chapter 11
1. Henry M. Morris, 1997, "Contending for the Faith," unpublished manuscript, 91.
2. Ibid, 94.

Chapter 12
1. Henry M. Morris, letter dated August 7, 1957.
2. Henry M. Morris, 1997, "Contending for the Faith," unpublished manuscript, 113.
3. Ibid, 115.
4. Ibid, 116.
5. Ibid, 134.
6. Ibid, 135-136.
7. Ibid, 138.
8. Presbyterian and Reformed Publishing Co. promotional pamphlet.
9. Ibid.
10. Morris, "Contending for the Faith," 140.
11. Presbyterian and Reformed Publishing Co. promotional pamphlet.
12. Morris, "Contending for the Faith," 118.
13. Henry M. Morris, 1984, *A History of Modern Creationism*, San Diego, CA: Master Book Publishers, 173-186.
14. Morris, "Contending for the Faith," 164.

Chapter 13
1. Henry M. Morris, 1997, "Contending for the Faith," unpublished manuscript, 171.
2. Ibid, 172.
3. Ibid.
4. Henry M. Morris, 1984, *A History of Modern Creationism*, San Diego, CA: Master Book Publishers, 236.
5. Ibid, 244.
6. Morris, "Contending for the Faith," 203.
7. Ibid, 203.
8. Ibid, 188.

Chapter 14
1. Henry M. Morris, 1984, *A History of Modern Creationism*, San Diego, CA: Master Book Publishers, 293.
2. Henry M. Morris, 1997, "Contending for the Faith," unpublished manuscript, 212.
3. Ibid.

4. Henry M. Morris, 1995, The Battle for True Education (III: ICR, For Such a Time as This), *Acts & Facts*, 24 (9).

5. Henry M. Morris, 1995, A Unique Creationist School of Science (V: ICR, For Such a Time as This), *Acts & Facts,* 24 (11).

6. Henry M. Morris, 1995, Reflections on Fifty Years in Creation Evangelism (I: ICR, For Such a Time as This), *Acts & Facts*, 24 (7).

Chapter 15

1. Henry M. Morris, 1997, "Contending for the Faith," unpublished manuscript, 262.

2. Henry M. Morris, 1989, "How a Christian Dies (A Home-Going of Andy Morris)," *Acts & Facts*, 18 (7).

3. Henry M. Morris, 2004, *For Time and Forever*, Green Forest, AR: Master Books, 205.

4. Henry M. Morris, 2006, *Some Call It Science: The Religion of Evolution*, Dallas, TX: Institute for Creation Research, 40-42.

5. Morris, *For Time and Forever*, 207.

About the Author

Dr. Henry M. Morris's youngest daughter, Rebecca Morris Barber, was raised in the beautiful town of Blacksburg, Virginia, and early on gained a deep appreciation for the wonder of God's creation. She and her husband, Don, began their ministry at a Bible camp, he as director, she as song leader and horseback riding instructor. Her ministry expanded to coaching various sports while homeschooling their three children. Eventually, her interest in nature and science led her to become certified as an herbalist to explore the natural remedies that God has provided for His creation. Today she and Don continue to be involved in the ministry of the Institute for Creation Research.

About ICR

In 1970, Dr. Henry M. Morris established the Institute for Creation Research to proclaim the scientific evidence that confirms the Bible. Almost a half-century later, ICR continues to debunk popular evolutionary claims and show that the Bible can be trusted on all matters—including origins and Earth history.

ICR Ph.D. scientists conduct research in genetics, geology, paleontology, anatomy, engineering, astrophysics, geophysics, nuclear physics, climatology, and other disciplines to bring greater understanding of God's wonderful creation. ICR hosts creation seminars, workshops, and conferences all over the nation, and provides training through the School of Biblical Apologetics (**ICR.edu**). ICR research is published in books, online news updates, and its central publication *Acts & Facts*, a full-color monthly magazine with a readership of over 250,000. ICR produces high-quality DVDs on topics related to science and the Bible. ICR radio programs and podcasts can be heard around the world.

Building on Dr. Morris' faithful legacy, ICR is now working on the ICR Discovery Center for Science and Earth History. The Discovery Center will proclaim God's truth in creation in ways never seen before! For more information on this latest endeavor, please visit **ICR.org/DiscoveryCenter.**

255